Homelands Revisited is a collection of memor
ex-students of Homelands Grammar School fc
over the first 20 years of its existence.

Dedicated to the

Homelands Grammar School
Old Girls' Association

H.O.G.A

NON
SINE PULVERE
PALMA

FOREWORD

As a co-executor of my late friend Marjorie Calow of Melbourne (1932-2016), I shared the task of finding good homes, where possible, for her many treasured possessions. This was not an easy job, as Marjorie kept absolutely everything, on top of having a mighty library of books, CDs, vinyl, periodicals and magazines.

So when I came face-to-face with the Honours Boards from Homelands, rescued by Marjorie from her alma mater some years ago, I was stumped. I didn't want to destroy them, but nor could we keep them, and nor did they have any real monetary value. So I resorted to social media and to my surprise found Kal's Homelands Facebook page. I was delighted when he came over to collect them, and even more pleased when he expressed an interest in reproducing *Homelands Remembered*, as compiled by Marjorie and her school contemporaries. I was able to pass on Marjorie's box of Homelands material and school photographs, all labelled and filed away in Marjorie's usual, meticulous manner.

Homelands held a very dear place in Marjorie's heart. As a student there in the 1940s she belonged to a generation where the chance of higher education for working class girls was still a novel thing, and Homelands provided an essential stepping stone towards it. She went on to graduate in Chemistry, with a subsequent career at Boots at Nottingham, though her real loves were literature and music. Her appreciation of the value of education was inherited from her father, and she later became a tutor organiser for the WEA (Workers' Educational Association), an organisation that her father had supported.

Marjorie felt, not altogether unreasonably, that the digital age was a threat to the printed word and archive material. Although she latterly used a word processor, she feared the misuse, corruption and destruction of digital data, and was deeply suspicious of online buying, banking or social media. She was an inveterate letter writer, and no fan of e-mail.

It's ironic, then, that the finding of a new outlet for Marjorie's Homelands research should be owed to the social media that she regarded with such suspicion. But she would be very pleased that it takes the form of a good old-fashioned book, and she would get great satisfaction from knowing that her efforts are still valued by the present generation. I only wish that she'd been alive to see it.

Philip Heath, Melbourne, February 2017

Last night I dreamt of Homelands....

Some of us occasionally dream about Homelands and some of us have sharp memories of our schooldays – or think we do. When seven "old girls", saddened by the closure of the school, took the decision to commit our memories to paper, independently and without collaboration, several of us remembered the same incidents, but from rather different perspectives. We have enjoyed producing this booklet and hope, at the very least, it will ensure our wonderful school is not totally forgotten.

Marjorie Calow

Marjorie Elizabeth Calow

January 3rd 1932 – March 12th 2016

NON SINE PULVERE PALMA

NO REWARD WITHOUT EFFORT

DARE TO TRY

~~NO PALMS WITHOUT DUST~~

If you want to get on, get a duster

Charles Herbert Aslin
CBE
F.R.I.B.A

15th December 1893 – 18th April 1959

Charles Herbert Aslin

Derby In Pictures - Mark Miley

Charles Herbert Aslin F.R.I.B.A. became the Borough Architect for Derby in 1929 and oversaw major changes in the layout of the town, known as the Central Improvement Plan (CIP).

He was also responsible for the design of a great many buildings of importance both within the CIP and elsewhere in the town. Unfortunately many of his buildings have been lost, but thankfully some do survive.

As with most towns in the UK, Derby had grown up haphazardly over the preceding centuries and by the early years of the twentieth century plans were being drawn up to create a more rational and coherent structure to parts of the town, particularly along the western bank of the River Derwent. Various plans were put forward after 1919 but all were to fall through, often due to a lack of money. However, in 1929 a plan was presented by C. H. Aslin, which was approved, although it was to be much revised before work began in 1931. The scheme involved the purchase and clearance of 12 acres of riverbank, redirecting a number of roads and creating a much improved crossing over the river.

Maxwell Craven in his *Illustrated History of Derby* states that there were four principle aims to the Central Improvement Plan. The first of these was to bring together the many departments of the council, which at that time were spread across the town. The second aim was to improve market facilities. At that time the markets covered part of the Morledge as well as the market square and frequently created traffic problems, particularly as the market square was still open to traffic at that time. As a result a large purpose-built outdoor market was to be created. The third part of the plan involved improvements to traffic flow, particularly diverting traffic from the heavily congested streets in the centre of the town. The final element was the already mentioned river crossing, which became Exeter Bridge.

Although financial problems in the 30s and the second world war meant that the whole scheme was never fully realised a great deal of it did go ahead. All along the river, Aslin constructed his buildings from the bus station through the outdoor market, council house, Exeter Bridge, police station and magistrates' court. Across the river he also built Exeter House, the regions first purpose built council flats. Elsewhere in the town he built the Queen Street Swimming Baths, which still survive although much altered, as well as a bandstand at the Arboretum and Homelands School, both of which have been lost.

On leaving Derby in 1945 Aslin became the County Architect for Hertfordshire and was at the forefront in the revolutionary development of prefabricated schools, something for which he is feted worldwide. His final achievement was to be elected President of the Royal Institute of British Architects in 1954.

History of Homelands

On September 9th 1938, Homelands School for Girls, the replacement for Central School for Girls, opened its classrooms on Village Street for the very first time.

Designed by the borough architect, C. H. Aslin, it cost nearly £46,000 and its staff would be responsible for the secondary education of some 490 pupils.

Although Charles Herbert Aslin was not actually born in Derby he did, in the year of the beginning of the BSAG campaign, manage a 'Hall Of Fame' nomination for an exhibition of achievement of local luminaries of the last Millennium, as reported on 30th November 1999 by Malcolm Bradbrook in the Derby Evening Telegraph. This was for his role as the Derby Borough Architect, who was in charge of the team that designed, not only the Bus Station itself, but also the Police Station/Magistrates' Courts, Council House, Riverside Gardens, Exeter Bridge, Exeter Place Apartments and the former Covered Market. This was all part of a ground-breaking, co-ordinated development called the 'Central Improvement Scheme' probably the most intact example of an inter-war regeneration scheme in existence in this country.

Aslin was actually born in Sheffield on 15th December 1893, the younger of two sons of Arthur William and Louisa Aslin, his father being a foreman in a Sheffield steelworks. C. H. Aslin received education first at Sheffield Central School then subsequently at Sheffield University. During World War I he was posted to the Army Pay Corps and the Oxford and Bucks, Light Infantry. From 1916 he held the rank of captain in the Royal Artillery and served on the Western Front until 1919.

Prior to enlisting, Aslin had passed the final examination of the Royal Institute of British Architects and in 1920 he was admitted as an associate, becoming a fellow in 1932. He began his employment in the architectural field on the staff of the city architect in Sheffield, then was appointed to the borough engineer in Rotherham, near Sheffield, in 1922, designing the new municipal offices. In the years immediately afterwards he was a lecturer at Sheffield University and became an associate of the Institution of Civil Engineers, also being appointed deputy county architect of Hampshire.

Aslin finally came to Derby in 1929, where, as described above, he designed his masterpiece. It is perhaps easy to be blasé about these city centre redevelopment schemes nowadays. However, one must not lose sight of the fact that, in its day, the C.I.S. was very much a pioneer piece of work.

Not satisfied with his work at Derby Borough Council alone, Aslin sought out pastures new after the conclusion of World War II, becoming county architect of Hertfordshire County Council. The previous year a new Education Act had come into force, which Aslin believed would create a demand for a new school building that would clearly exceed the capacity of traditional school building techniques. Hertfordshire was, in this respect, an ideal proving ground for Aslin's new concept of prefabricated construction techniques. The County Council were encouraging in their attitude towards this new venture, but there were some in the architectural trade who were decidedly suspicious of its efficacy.

In the event Aslin was entirely vindicated and his Hertfordshire schools became as much a place of pilgrimage as Derby Bus Station had been a decade-and-a-half or so previously. Some ten or so years later one hundred of these schools had been built and the hundredth example thereof was opened by the minister for education. Furthermore, the system he had evolved had been emulated by all local authorities in the land. Aslin had been an outstanding team leader, in charge of a team made up of some of the best and brightest in the business and it was not a hard job attracting those of that sort of calibre, since jobs in his office were some of the most sought after in the country.

Taking a step outside Aslin's bare architectural achievements, from 1941–43 he was president of the Notts, Derby and Lincoln Society of Architects and was their representative on the council of the R.I.B.A. A key achievement at the R.I.B.A. was the harmonisation of pay and conditions between architects in private practice and those in salaried positions, the latter of which were dissatisfied with those conditions. In 1945, Aslin was elected in his own right to the council of the R.I.B.A. and in 1954–56 was president. In his presidential address he stressed the importance of making the architectural profession more efficient and of giving better service to the client and public. He was awarded the C.B.E. in 1951. In addition to this, Aslin was an associate of the Institution of Structural Engineers, a member of the Royal Society of Arts, honorary fellow of the American Institute of Architects and R.I.B.A. bronze medallist (1951).

Aslin's circle of friends was wide and varied, in terms of age, background and race. Together with his shrewd, north-country nature, this enabled him to take a firm stand when a serious matter arose and also to take a very dim view of pomposity and pretension. Throughout his life he had the support of his wife, (Ethel Fawcett Armitage, also of Sheffield, married in 1920, with whom he had one daughter) without whom, he admitted, he would never have attained his full potential. Outside of his professional life he was a good tennis player and had a keen interest in both cricket and the theatre. He was an accomplished photographer, was widely read and was a supporter of numerous societies. During World War II he contributed a great deal to Anglo–Polish relations. Although he was brought up as a strict Non-Conformist he later joined the Church of England and was a man of strong religious principles.

Aslin narrowly escaped death in 1955 when his room filled with gas as a result of a fractured main and it is thought that this ultimately may have led indirectly to his eventual death in Hertford on 18th April 1959, the year following his retirement.

His portrait, by Allan Gwynne Jones, can be seen at the headquarters of the R.I.B.A.

The aforementioned information on Aslin's life and work is courtesy of S. Morrison by way of the Dictionary of National Biography: 1951–1960.

C. H. ASLIN

ORDNANCE SURVEY MAP

1937–1961

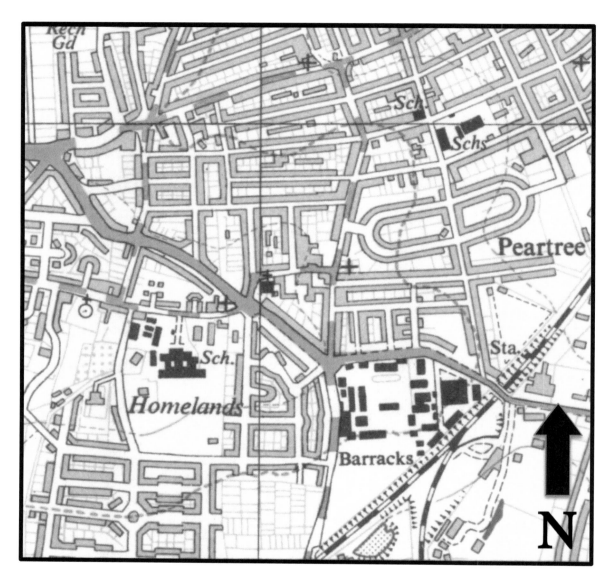

Normanton – Derby
© 2016 National Library of Scotland

SCHOOL PLAN

1938

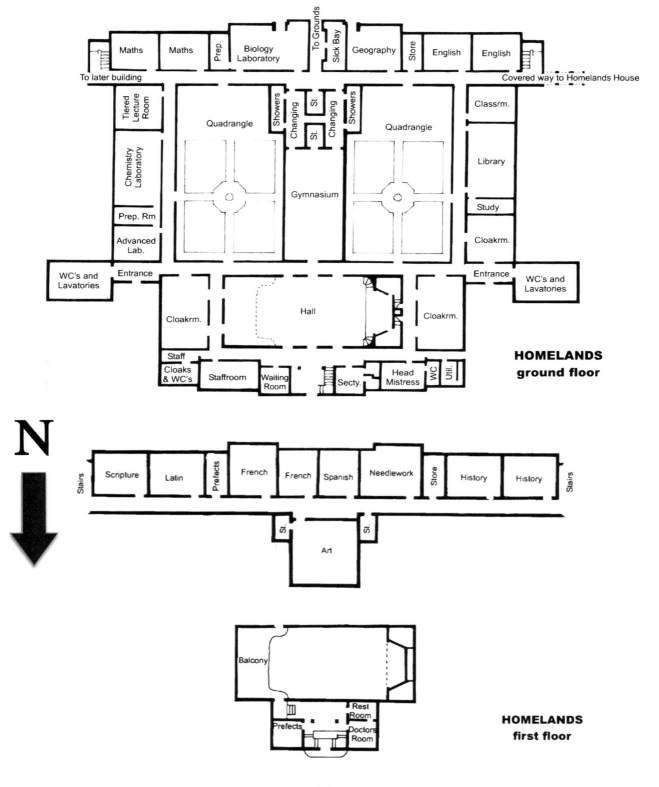

WORK STARTS AT NEW HOMELANDS
SCHOOL FOR GIRLS

DERBY EVENING TELEGRAPH, THURSDAY, SEPTEMBER 15, 1938.

WORK STARTS AT NEW HOMELANDS SCHOOL FOR GIRLS

Pupils of the Homelands Secondary School for Girls, Normanton, which was officially opened last Friday, assembled at their new school for the first time yesterday, and here they are listening to an address by their headmistress, Miss M. E. Welbank.

Photograph courtesy of Derby Evening Telegraph

Miss Mary E. Welbank
Headmistress

Homelands Grammar School for Girls, Village Street

Derbyshire Advertiser, 25th June 1937

The foundation stone of Derby's new secondary school for girls was laid by the Mayor of Derby, Councillor Mrs E. Petty, on 23 June 1937 and marked an important stage in Derby's educational development. The school, which will be known as "Homelands", is estimated to cost £45,750 to provide ten classrooms including a geography room for 30 pupils in each and three classrooms for 20 pupils in each.

"Speaking to the girls, Alderman Dr H. H. Bemrose, Chairman of the Ceremony, said it was, he believed, the first time in Derby that the whole of the girls from the Central School had been present at the laying of a foundation stone. It was the foundation stone of a school to which they would migrate in a few years and they would then not enter a central school but a secondary school, one which would provide further educational facilities. They would be trained for work, for leisure and for responsibility."

The Mayor laid the foundation stone and the Reverend R. G. McAlpine (Vicar of St Giles's) said the dedication prayer.

Mrs Petty 'went on to speak of the wonderful view those at the school would have across the Vale of Trent. Such a glorious vista would inspire them all the time they were at work. The Mayor concluded by wishing true success to the school and its future and to the staff that would be working there.'

The Opening ceremony of the new school was performed in September 1938 by Miss Margaret Keay, MBE, formerly a head at Abbey Street Central School and the first head of Parkfields School.

The school was designed by Mr C. H. Aslin, Borough Architect, and it was reported that 'his vision was of a school amongst the trees and that is a good description of Homelands as we have it today.'

Mr Aslin, commenting on the school 'explained that the entrance to the school faced north and the assembly hall opened directly upon the entrance hall. There were 13 classrooms, two chemistry laboratories, physics and biology laboratories, lecture room, library, geography room, needlework room and an art room. There was a gymnasium with shower baths and changing rooms, headmistress' room and staff rooms. The school was connected to a domestic science block by a covered way and a dining room was provided in this block.'

There were two quadrangles, Mr Aslin added, 'not at their best as yet but designed to add to the amenities of the school'. They would, he thought, 'be found very pleasant'.

The whole of the classrooms were on the south side of the school and looked over the Vale of Trent to Breedon-on-the-Hill. The assembly hall had a fully equipped stage, with head lights, foot lights, etc. The school would accommodate 490 children. The sum of £2,850 had been spent on the furniture, all of which, with the exception of the chairs, had been specially designed.

The initial intake of pupils on 14 September 1938 was 380 – with 19 members of staff. By the time of the 'coming of age' of the school, in September 1959, there were 608 pupils, 29 full-time members of staff and three part-time members. By this time, too, some additions had been made to the original buildings and new laboratories were badly needed.

To commemorate the occasion each form in the school was to provide a tree for planting in the school grounds – 21 of them altogether. However, due to the dry summer of that year, only three trees were planted at a token ceremony. The first tree was planted by Alderman A. Sturgess, chairman of the school governors and present at the laying of the foundation stone. The Director of Education, Mr Charles Middleton, planted the second tree and the third tree was planted jointly by Celia Winterton and Margaret Parker, previous and present head girls. A service of thanksgiving was held in the Cathedral in mid-September and attended by the present pupils, staff, parents and others associated with the school over the first 21 years.

By now pupils were being educated up to the age of 18 years of age, or to 16 if they wished.

In the corner of the playing fields, close to Kitchener Avenue, a temporary building was erected during World War Two to accommodate a day nursery. Use of the building continued until it was finally demolished in the 1970s.

Normanton-by-Derby Local History Group

Normanton Secondary School, Village Street

An event which celebrated the Centenary of the 1870 Education Act was the official Opening on 21 September 1970, of Normanton Secondary School. This school, initially with an entrance off Arleston Street, was constructed alongside the Homelands building so as to replace the Old Pear Tree Boys' and Girls' Schools in Harrington and Portland Streets. This school was one of the first six buildings in the County over three storeys high and designed in the CLASP system – a construction technique developed in Nottinghamshire and Derbyshire. This system reduced the time taken in design and construction.

The site available for building was extremely limited and it was felt that the fine views from the site should not be obscured and also that existing trees should be preserved but leaving as much room as possible for playing field purposes. The principal teaching spaces were to be accommodated in a four-storey tower block. The value of Phase I of the work was £242,000 with an additional £17,500 being added for Phase II, which consisted of further accommodation. Between 580 and 600 students were to be taught. A feature on the outside of the building near the main entrance, which was designed by Mr J.T. Glover, the art master of the school, is a mural in concrete.

Image courtesy of K. S. Dhindsa © 2007

Homelands Comprehensive School

By 1972, comprehensive education was introduced to Derby, and Homelands Grammar School and Normanton Secondary School merged to create the larger Homelands Comprehensive, which, of course, became co-educational at the same time. An opportunity was also taken to reorganise the catchment areas of the schools in the town. A segment starting from the centre of town and spreading out towards the boundary of the Borough was to be the new catchment of Homelands necessitating a fairly long journey to school for some pupils.

Regrettably, the first half of the 1980s was marred by damage by fire, arson attacks and the discovery of asbestos in the buildings.

Village Community School

By September 1989, the County Education Committee had decided to reorganise secondary education in the city and to create sixth-form colleges. Therefore, teaching at the schools was to be up to the age of 16 years with any further tuition being continued in one of the two further education colleges in the city.

The opportunity was taken at this time to change the name of Homelands Comprehensive School to the Village Community School.

Village High School

In September 2001 Village Community School then became known as Village High School. Village High remained open for less than a year before it was finally closed down for good in June 2002.

Not long after that, Charles Herbert Aslin's beautiful Hastings building was knocked down and lost forever.

Village Primary School

In September 2008, 70 years after Homelands Grammar School for Girls first opened it's doors, a new school by the name of Village Primary School began welcoming a new generation of children at the old Homelands site.

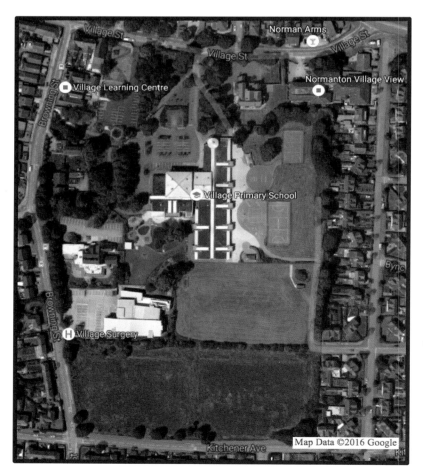

Original School Houses

Sir Richard

Arkwright

23rd December 1732 – 3rd August 1792

Anthony

Babington

24th October 1561 – 20th September 1586

Charles Robert

Darwin

12th February 1809 – 19th April 1882

Florence

Nightingale

12th May 1820 – 13th August 1910

Herbert

Spencer

27th April 1820 – 8th December 1903

Each House was named after a prominent person with local connections
Image source: Wikipedia

Sir Richard Arkwright was born at Preston in 1732, the youngest of 13 children of a labourer. His family could not afford education, but arranged for him to be taught to read and write by his cousin. He initially became an apprentice to a barber, and travelled the country seeking human hair for the manufacture of wigs. While on his travels he heard about the attempts being made to produce new machines for the textile industry.

John Kay, a clockmaker from Warrington, had been working with Thomas Highs of Leigh, but they had soon run out of money.

Arkwright was so impressed by Kay that he offered to employ them both to make a new machine, the Spinning Frame. However, Arkwright's Spinning Frame was too large to be operated by hand so an alternative method had to be found.

After experimenting with horses it was decided to employ the power of the waterwheel and in 1771 the three men set up a large factory next to the River Derwent in Cromford, Derbyshire. This machine became known as Arkwright's Water Frame.

The invention of the Spinning Jenny and Spinning Frame caused an increase in the demand for cardings and rovings. Lewis Paul had invented a machine for carding in 1748. Arkwright made improvements in this machine and in 1775 took out a patent for a new Carding Engine. In 1767 he attempted to solve the problem of perpetual motion and, soon after, with the help of Kay, his spinning inventions began to take shape. He then entered into partnership with a firm of stocking manufacturers, and his invention was patented in 1769.

Though many difficulties arose, from infringements of the patent, the hostility of the work-people, and disputes to his claim as the inventor of his machines, Arkwright was enabled to rise from poverty, and was chosen to present a congratulatory address to George III in 1786, on which occasion he was Knighted. He died in 1792.

Anthony Babington was a very rich Catholic landowner who lived in Derbyshire. He is famous for plotting with Mary Queen of Scots with the intention of putting the Catholic Queen on the throne of England in place of the Protestant, Elizabeth I.

Mary used a code to communicate with Babington in the mistaken belief that the code was secure, but the chief of the Security Services, Walsingham broke the code. However, although indiscreet, Mary did not give the names of the conspirators, so Walsingham arranged that a final paragraph was added to one of Mary's letters by using the code and copying Mary's handwriting, asking Babington to tell her the names. This he did in reply. All the conspirators were then rounded up and executed at Tyburn in 1586.

In death, Anthony Babington's family became so ashamed by what he had done that they changed the family name, so there are now various versions: e.g. Bebbington and Bebington.

Charles Robert Darwin was a British Naturalist.

In 1859 he published *The Origin of the Species*. This book concerned his Theory of Natural Selection.

'I have called this principle, by which each slight variation, if useful, is preserved, by the term Natural Selection'

Charles Darwin was born in Shrewsbury, England. He was the fifth child and second son of Robert Waring Darwin and Susannah Wedgwood. Darwin became famous for his theories of evolution and natural selection. Like several scientists before him, Darwin believed all the life on earth evolved (developed gradually) over millions of years from a few common ancestors.

From 1831 to 1836 Darwin served as a naturalist aboard the H.M.S. Beagle on a British science expedition around the world. In South America, Darwin found fossils of extinct animals that were similar to modern species. On the Galapagos Islands, in the Pacific Ocean, he noticed many variations among plants and animals of the same general type as those in South America. The expedition visited places around the world, and Darwin studied plants and animals everywhere he went, collecting specimens for further study.

Upon his return to London Darwin conducted thorough research of his notes and specimens. Out of this study grew several related theories: one, evolution did occur; two, evolutionary change was gradual, requiring thousands to millions of years; three, the primary mechanism for evolution was a process called natural selection; and four, the millions of species alive today arose from a single original life form through a branching process called 'specialization'.

Darwin's theory of evolutionary selection holds that variation within species occurs randomly and that the survival or extinction of each organism is determined by that organism's ability to adapt to its environment. He set these theories forth in his book called, *On the Origin of Species by Means of Natural Selection, or the Preservation of Favoured Races in the Struggle for Life* (1859). After publication, Darwin continued to write on botany, geology, and zoology until his death in 1882. He is buried in Westminster Abbey.

Darwin's work had a tremendous impact on religious thought. Many people strongly opposed the idea of evolution because it conflicted with their religious convictions. Darwin avoided talking about the theological and sociological aspects of his work, but other writers used his theories to support their own theories about society. Darwin was a reserved, thorough, hard-working scholar who concerned himself with the feelings and emotions, not only of his family, but friends and peers as well.

It has been supposed that Darwin renounced evolution on his deathbed. Shortly after his death, temperance campaigner and evangelist Lady Elizabeth Hope claimed she visited Darwin at his deathbed, and witnessed the renunciation. Her story was printed in a Boston newspaper and subsequently spread. Lady Hope's story was refuted by Darwin's daughter Henrietta who stated, 'I was present at his deathbed. He never recanted any of his scientific views, either then or earlier'.

Florence Nightingale lived at Lea Hurst in Lea near Holloway. An English social reformer and statistician, and the founder of modern nursing.

'I attribute my success to this – I never gave or took any excuse.'

She is best remembered for her work as a nurse during the Crimean War and her contribution towards the reform of the sanitary conditions in military field hospitals.

'I think one's feelings waste themselves in words; they ought all to be distilled into actions which bring results.'

For most of her ninety years, Nightingale pushed for reform of the British military healthcare system and with that the profession of nursing started to gain the respect it deserved. Unknown to many, however, was her use of new techniques of statistical analysis, such as during the Crimean War when she plotted the incidence of preventable deaths in the military. She developed the 'polar-area diagram' to dramatize the needless deaths caused by unsanitary conditions and the need for reform. With her analysis, Florence Nightingale revolutionised the idea that social phenomena could be objectively measured and subjected to mathematical analysis. She was an innovator in the collection, tabulation, interpretation, and graphical display of descriptive statistics.

Florence Nightingale's two greatest life achievements pioneering of nursing and the reform of hospitals, were amazing considering that most Victorian women of her age group did not attend universities or pursue professional careers. It was her father, William Nightingale, who believed women, especially his children, should get an education. So, Nightingale and her sister learned Italian, Latin, Greek, history, and mathematics. She, in particular, received excellent early preparation in mathematics from her father and aunt, and was also tutored in mathematics by James Sylvester. In 1854, after a year as an unpaid superintendent of a London 'establishment for gentlewomen during illness,' the Secretary of War, Sidney Herbert, recruited Nightingale and thirty-eight nurses for service in Scutari during the Crimean War.

During Nightingale's time at Scutari, she collected data and systematised record-keeping practices. Nightingale was able to use the data as a tool for improving city and military hospitals. Nightingale's calculations of the mortality rate showed that with an improvement of sanitary methods, deaths would decrease. In February 1855, the mortality rate at the hospital was 42.7 per cent of the cases treated. When Nightingale's sanitary reform was implemented, the mortality rate declined. Nightingale took her statistical data and represented them graphically. She invented polar-area charts, where the statistic being represented is proportional to the area of a wedge in a circular diagram.

As Nightingale demonstrated, statistics provided an organised way of learning and lead to improvements in medical and surgical practices. She also developed a Model Hospital Statistical Form for hospitals to collect and generate consistent data and statistics.

Florence Nightingale

Herbert Spencer was born in Derby and was a privately educated, English philosopher, biologist, anthropologist, sociologist, and prominent classical liberal political theorist of the Victorian era.

'Science is organised knowledge.'

He is best known for the expression 'Survival of the fittest', which he coined in *Principles of Biology* (1864), after reading Charles Darwin's *On the Origin of Species by Means of Natural Selection, or the Preservation of Favoured Races in the Struggle for Life* (1859).

'In science the important thing is to modify and change one's ideas as science advances.'

His father was a schoolteacher and Herbert was the only child of his parents to live beyond early childhood. His early interests were science, natural history, physics and chemistry. At the age of 16, he completed his formal education and was an Assistant Schoolmaster. Later he became a railroad engineer working for nine years for the London and Birmingham Railway. He gained a reputation as a philosopher, but later, scientists proved many of his theories wrong.

In 1852, Herbert Spencer wrote an article defending the theory of biological evolution, a full seven years before Charles Darwin published *On the Origin of Species by Means of Natural Selection, or the Preservation of Favoured Races in the Struggle for Life*. His view of evolution encompassed all of nature; the biological model being the basis for understanding the social model. It was Spencer who first used such terms as 'system', 'function', and 'structure'.

He is noted for his attempt to work out a philosophy based on scientific discoveries of his day, which could be applied to all subjects. In *Programme of a System of Synthetic Philosophy* (1862, 1896), he applied his fundamental law: the idea of evolution (gradual development) to biology, psychology, sociology, and other fields.

In his work on biology, he traced evolutionary development from its lowest forms to human beings. He believed that the law of nature is a constant action of forces, which tend to change all forms from simple to complex. He also explained that the human mind evolved in this same way, from simple automatic responses to the reasoning process used by human beings today.

Spencer most resembled the eighteenth century philosophers in his attempt to apply the implications of science to social thought and action. He felt that the ultimate result of universal evolution was 'equilibration' or the achievement of a state of perfect equilibrium, whether it was in the development of an animal organism or within human society. In an organism, the equilibrium was represented by decay and death, where development ended. However, in a society, this process ended with the establishment of perfection and happiness.

Joy (née Bezant) Bastien

I certainly remember my first day at Homelands in September 1938. I felt I was lucky to be one of the first at the new school as I was only nine years old – ten at the end of October – and the deadline for entry in that year was two days after my birthday. Being the youngest in the school meant I had to present a bouquet at the first Speech Day, I believe to the Mayoress.

I remember the barrage balloons and aircrew in the front garden and the fact that we had to attend school part of the time while the air raid shelters were being completed.

I went to a farming camp at Shottle and picked potatoes, but mostly I remember 'stooking' wheat, which was always wet and nasty and often the stooks collapsed and had to be reassembled. One year there was so much rain that the tents leaked and we all had to sleep in the cow byres at the farm, on our lumpy straw filled palliases, with the bull pacing below all through the night.

Whilst we were there, my mother and Rosemary Harrison's mother came out by bus to see us and took us to the guest house at Idridgehay where we had boiled eggs (from their own hens) and brown bread and butter – a rare treat in the days of rationing. I look at the farm machinery in use today and think back to those back-breaking days at Shottle, but I think we all enjoyed them.

I remember all the teachers, I suppose most particularly Miss Moore, who was my form teacher when I started. A few years later she came to lodge next door to me in Grange Avenue (and opposite Rosemary and Moyra Harrison). Unfortunately, she used the front room downstairs as a lounge and kept a close eye on what we did in the evenings, mentioning on more than one occasion to my mother that I really ought to be doing some more revision instead of being out on my bicycle.

I seem to recall that we had to learn all the national anthems of the Allies to sing at Speech Day during the war.

Joan (née Allsop) Frost

I have one particular memory of my first week at Homelands in 1938. At assembly, the Head (Miss Welbank) announced that no one was to walk across the west Quadrangle during break due to exams in the library. Having only been there a few days we didn't know our way around the school let alone east from west. So it came to pass that three friends and myself were met by Miss Vera Land (Hilda's sister) as we walked across the West Quadrangle. The outcome of this terrible crime was '500' lines – 'I must learn to do as I am told'. My parents were not pleased.

I must learn to do as I am told

I must learn to do as I am told

I must learn to do as I am told

I must learn to do as I am told

I must learn to do as I am told

I must learn to do as I am told

I must learn to do as I am told

I must learn to do as I am told

I must learn to do as I am told

I must learn to do as I am told

I must learn to do as I am told

I must learn to do as I am told

I must learn to do as I am told

I must learn to do as I am told

Rosemary (née Harrison) Speakman

I started my time there in 1938 when the school opened. I can remember on my first day that the girls who had come from Hastings Street School were already at 'prayers' in the Hall, they were singing the hymn 'He who would valiant be' I thought it sounded absolutely wonderful and I remember the sound of it to this day.

I remember Miss Pakeman who taught maths, she seemed very old to me, as she taught my mother at Hastings Street School.

Also, if we were not looking at her as she spoke she would say, 'I want your eyes' or 'Give me your eyes' – most alarming!

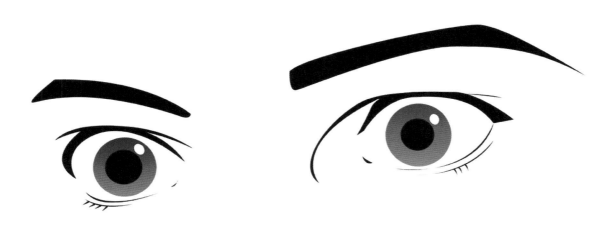

For the last year or two that I was at Homelands I had Miss Yates for French. She also wanted you to listen to every word she said – and why not?

I also seem to remember that there was a barrage balloon anchored in front of the school in the early days of the war.

Also, I remember that there were GIs waiting for some of the older girls at the school, outside.

Another memory is of going to Shottle on a train with other school friends to work on Mr Fletcher's farm for two weeks. We had bell tents in one of his fields.

Audrey (née Fenton) King

I was so pleased to go to Homelands and soon made friends. My close friend was Marion Compton, who said she would help me with Maths if I could help her with art! Art being one of my favourite subjects.

English, French, Art, Sport I looked forward to – Friday afternoons were bliss – double Art and French.

I liked Miss Hughes, but I felt a bit mortified when, with a twinkle in her eye, she asked me to remove a bit of chewing gum and come to the front of the class to recite a poem called 'Daffodils'.

I wasn't awfully keen on Geography or Miss Thompson, but will always remember her saying that one member of the class needed her bottom smacked. I turned to Pat Shepherd and said, 'I wonder who that is?' In a thunderous voice Miss Thompson said, 'Audrey Fenton – it is you!!!'

However, I always seemed to be trotting to Miss Welbank with my 'good' written work.

I was the first of the Fenton families to go to Homelands. My cousin Joyce Fenton followed me, then my sister Pamela Fenton, then my daughter Sally King. Halfway through Sally's years the school became a comprehensive one, which disappointed me. However, Sally went on to get a degree in Psychology, and is still working in the educational field.

I am so pleased that we can enjoy our 'get togethers'.

Winifred (née Eales) Curzon

My recollections date from September 1938 when I was privileged to enter the pristine school building as a member of the first form.

We had a very pleasant first year and were looking forward to being second year pupils with a new intake below us. However, World War II began on September 3rd 1939. Parents of my year were advised that because the building of air-raid shelters in the grounds would take some time, our year's return would be delayed by a month. Our year was considered the best group to miss some schooling as we had already received a grounding in the school system and unlike the older girls were not about to embark on an examination syllabus. Form 2 pupils were encouraged to stay in the country – away from the likely action. My friend Margaret Lloyd and I stayed in Brailsford with my aunt and uncle on their farm for four weeks.

Air-raid Warning Drill – When the school bell rang continuously we had to stop activity immediately and make our way in an orderly fashion by a prescribed route to an air raid shelter and must not delay to pick up personal items, apart from our gas mask.

The member of staff whose lesson had been interrupted allowed us to sing. I remember being in Miss Thompson's Geography class when the ominous bell sounded. The geography room had French windows, which provided access to the shelters without using corridors. Miss Thompson was so scared – she told the girls to let her out first and to follow when all the doors and windows were closed. Of course we obeyed. When we arrived in the shelter Miss T. was already there, quaking. She asked us to keep quiet and not to sing so that she could hear whether there were enemy planes about and whether any bombs were dropped. The most embarrassing aspect of the near silence was when a pupil used the elsan in front of all her form mates.

I give full marks to the staff of Homelands School for the education I received in the period 1938–45. Miss Welbank left Homelands when I did so I did not experience Dorothea Susannah Gilbert – a one-day wonder. I attended reunions when Miss Helmore was Head.

I made some good friends at Homelands and have kept in touch with eight of them. The Reunions have been good and I look forward to attending more.

Patricia (née Shepard) Cooper

I went to Homelands school in September 1938 when it first opened. I started in form 1C and Miss Moore was our form mistress. She took us for English, history and R.E. In English we had to write a composition every week and it had to consist of three paragraphs. We also had to learn a piece of poetry every week and recite it in front of the class! In history we learnt about the Greeks and Romans and had to draw the three types of Roman columns – Corinthian, Ionic and Doric – information, which I have never forgotten!

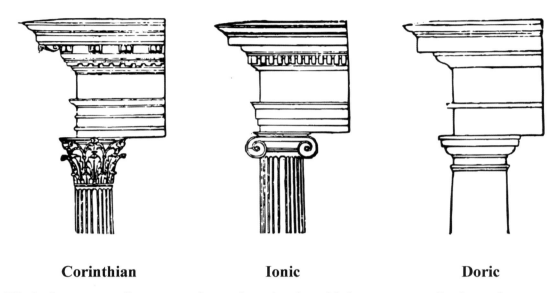

Corinthian   **Ionic**   **Doric**

We had to cover all our exercise and textbooks with brown paper. In those days most people would have a stash of brown paper at home because all purchases were put into paper bags or wrapped in large sheets of brown paper and tied with string. (Plastic and Sellotape had not been invented.) Sometimes if brown paper was not available left over pieces of wallpaper were used and dirty covers could be given a new lease of life by turning inside out and refolding. Woe betide anyone who did not cover their books!

One of the first things we made during our first year in Needlework was a needlecase – made in green material and the front was decorated with various stitches (our own design) and a sample of darning (who darns anything today?!). I have always been keen on dressmaking and embroidery and I used this same needlecase until 1976 when, after my mother's death, I inherited the contents of her sewing drawer and found a much superior needlecase. I didn't feel too guilty about throwing the old one out after 38 years of constant use! During the mid 1950s I made friends with a neighbour and one day, when I was at her home, I saw a needlecase, which could only have come from one place. On enquiring – yes she had been at Homelands though not my year but the needlecase had not changed one iota!

In spite of wartime restrictions, rules about uniform were quite strict and tunics had to be a regulation length (checked regularly by Miss Land, our P.E. teacher). Hats were worn in summer and winter!

There was a barrage balloon tethered on the triangle of grass in front of the school. After the initial interest had died down it became part of our daily lives and I don't think we took much notice of it. I don't remember any daytime raids while I was at school but I do remember occasional air-raid practices when we had to go and sit in the underground shelters built in the grounds at the back of the school.

British military auxiliaries handle a barrage balloon

Operation Outward – Image Source: Wikipedia

The all-female staff were <u>all</u> single ladies in 1938. Married teachers were not employed in those days. I only remember one married teacher who joined the staff during the latter part of the war. We respected the teachers and called them by their surnames (Miss Moore etc.).

My memories of most of the staff put them definitely in the 'middle age' bracket and I'm amazed how young some of them look! Just goes to show what a wrong impression of their elders children have.

As part of our P.E. lessons we learnt country and ballroom dancing (old fashioned waltz, quick-step etc.) and we had Christmas parties when the pupils had to dance with each other and with the staff! When we reached the VI form we were allowed to join the Derby School boys at St Helen's House for Xmas dances!

I think we enjoyed our school days – I know I did. There was no bullying, no drugs, no playing truant and I never heard of anyone getting pregnant while still at school.

Needless to say we had no calculators or computers and the knowledge of tables was essential – that knowledge has stood in good stead all my life.

Margaret (née Foxon) Handley

In September 1938 Homelands School opened its doors and I entered as Second Former, along with all those who had spent our year as First Formers at the Central School in Hastings Street. What a contrast between the old Central School building and this beautiful brand new school with the pleasant well-laid out approach from the main gate and inside everything so new. It was all so wonderful, and a little bit bewildering. There was the school hall with the stage, with real theatre curtains and stage lighting, the well equipped gym, the new classrooms with modern desks (remember the yellow boards and blue chalk?) the lovely playing fields and the pleasant surroundings.

I remember the talk Miss Welbank gave us, reminding us all how very fortunate we were to have this lovely new school and that we must all take care not to spoil it.

There was a barrage balloon at the front of the school, air-raid shelters on the top playing fields and protective netting over the windows. We were encouraged to 'do our bit' to help the war effort, such as 'digging for victory' in the kitchen garden, and knitting comforts such as mittens, scarves and balaclava helmets for the troops.

DIG FOR VICTORY !

As we progressed up the school we were able to do more to help the war effort. The Homelands Service Corps was formed and we learned useful, practical things like First Aid. Occasionally we were allowed to help at the Forces canteen in the town. For some this was something of a disappointment as we were kept strictly in the kitchen and not allowed to serve the cups of tea etc. to members of H.M. Forces seeking refreshment there. Approaching Christmas, when exams were over, some of us helped with sorting the mail at the main sorting office. There were days when we helped on nearby farms, planting cabbages and potatoes, and in the summer holidays some of us camped at Shottle Hall Farm and helped with harvesting there and on surrounding farms; stocking wheat, helping with threshing, treading silage and so on. Who remembers Miss Yates driving over on the occasion of the liberation of Paris, overjoyed at the news and asking to sing the Marseillaise after supper that evening?

There are many happy memories of those days at Homelands. The inter-house competitions, the concerts and plays put on by various forms at the end of term. There were friendships formed, some of which have lasted over the years.

I remember many of the staff with affection and gratitude. To name them all would take too long on this occasion, but led by Miss Welbank they worked with dedication and I am grateful to them.

Joan (née Wilby) Patterson

It all seems a very long time ago! My memory 'plays me tricks' nowadays, too, and I've made little effort to sort out when things happened.

Those of us who started in the Central School looked forward so much to going to the grammar school that I am surprised I cannot remember the first day. My classmates, many of the teachers, and our headmistress, Miss Welbank were of course old friends.

The school building was most impressive – a large hall, a gym, with showers! A lecture hall, a science lab, a sick bay, lots of classrooms with new furniture, a library. We were very surprised to find heaters in the ceiling in the science lab we knew that heat rises so that didn't seem to make sense. We started to learn physics, and chemistry and biology (albeit as part of a general science course) and not just botany. I was the one in my group who was persuaded to wield the knife to dissect a fish. The next thing I knew I was lying on a bed in the sick bay.

From 1939, of course, we were at war and life did change, although Derby did not suffer as much as we feared. At school we practised what to do if there was an air-raid warning, although I cannot recall the sirens during the daytime.

I lived very close to Rolls-Royce and the railway carriage works but the camouflage was so good, that very often the aeroplanes passed overhead, and dropped their bombs elsewhere. An air-raid shelter at the gates of Rolls-Royce was hit one morning and some people we knew were killed, including a few ex-pupils from Homelands. Nights were often spent in the Anderson shelter in the garden.

'Ludwig Siegfried', the Luftwaffe Dornier plane that carried out the 1942 raid on Derby's Rolls-Royce

Photograph courtesy of Derby Evening Telegraph

At school we had lessons in the school hall for a while, morning or afternoon. All I really remember was singing songs from the Mikado and the like. There was a barrage balloon at the front of the school and we were supposed to walk up the left-hand side of the drive so as not to speak to the RAF men in charge! Public exams, School Certificate and Higher School Certificate were at times a nightmare. I recall on several occasions putting my head down on the desk in despair after a sleepless night. Somehow we got through and the results for most of us were as expected. At my last Speech Day, Noel Baker presented the prizes and I remember how friendly he was as we chatted over refreshments in the library.

I got friendly with Frankie Sennett who joined us from London for a while; so much more sophisticated and worldly wise than most of us and so self confident. Seems unbelievable now that Miss Jewsbury came to London with me when I went for an interview at Bedford College, London University. I opted for Manchester in the end. I met Miss Welbank in London after I started teaching and in retirement she was doing some social work. I have never forgotten her saying, 'Joan, I never knew how the other half of the world lived'.

One day a week, I assume, we stayed behind after school. I don't remember what we called ourselves (Homelands Service Corps?) but we learned some First Aid, collected nettles for making wine without being stung – a lesson which has been very useful through the years. We knitted gloves and socks and wrote letters to the service men. I believe the school adopted a ship and we made up parcels at Christmas. Even at the time I remember we did not seem to be doing much to help the war effort!

We played hockey, netball and tennis and did some athletics but there were no sports days. We dressed up for dances and had 'cards' showing our partners and were expected to have some dances with members of staff!! I am sure we had some plays and concerts. I do remember our farm camps and staying in village halls, sleeping on straw palliasses on the floor. We worked in the fields stocking sheaves of corn which I found very satisfying, although very tiring.

The netball team at Homelands Grammar School, Derby, in 1938–39

Photograph courtesy of Derby Evening Telegraph

36

I am in touch with no one from school now except my cousins, Beryl and Betty Walker, and was disappointed in 1988 not to meet anyone from my form. I have mentioned Miss Welbank and Miss Jewsbury and other teachers I knew well were Mrs Yates, Pakeman, Hughes, Steele, Moore, Bennett, Miss Land who took P.E. and frequently checked the length of our tunics and the other Miss Land, her sister. Of Miss Fowler who came from Cambridge to teach us English, I remember only the nickname.

Miss Jewsbury   Miss Bennett

Miss Steele   Miss Yates   Miss Wilkins   Miss Newman   Miss Elliott

Photographs courtesy of Jacquie (née Ashmole) Weston

Sheila G (née Thompson) Samways

Joined Form 2A 1938

On reflection, what I remember most clearly is a happy school with totally dedicated staff and I don't recall any of the bickering, spitefulness and bullying that seems prevalent in schools today. Perhaps it is another case of 'the sun was always shining'.

Needlework

Much has been made of Bucko's Baggy Bloomers and the needlework cases but does anyone remember the equally baggy pyjamas? Mine were blue with pink flowers and were too hideous to wear even in those days of clothing shortage, however they came into their own some ten years later when heavily pregnant with my first child they finally were a fit. So much for the 5 inch 'rise' at the back!

I hated the tedium of Miss Buckley's needlework classes, the endless tacking and 'stroking' gathers, the hemming pulled out time after time until she was quite satisfied but I have over the years been more than grateful for the skills she passed on, and the tips 'for a blood spot chew a piece of cotton and then rub the spot with it, something in the saliva neutralises the blood'. That one came in useful twenty or more years later whilst sewing same daughter's wedding dress.

Homework

During the war some of the teachers stayed after school to supervise girls who preferred to do their homework at school. This must have been entirely voluntary but was a great help to girls like me whose homes lacked the necessary quiet corner. I think Wednesday night was free and we could get a cup of tea in the dining room before sitting down to work at 4.30, leaving at 6 or 6.30 pm. I often wondered why more girls did not stay; there were only two classrooms in use as I recall.

War effort

I remember those of us who had bikes, going out with Miss Elliott to collect foxgloves along the hedgerows by Mugginton Lane End, for the digitalis presumably. I don't remember whether it was the flowers or the leaves but I know the sun was shining. We had First Aid classes and that was when I first saw myself as Florence Nightingale. It only took six months to prove me wrong a few years later. I also spent several days writing names on Ration Books, but I can't remember how that came about. In 1939 we had morning lessons one week and afternoon lessons the next so we had a complete timetable every fortnight with extra homework to keep us busy on the half days we were at home. This went on until enough shelters had been built.

The School

Heaven after the cramped accommodation at Hastings St. It smelled of polish and fresh air and there were roses on the pillars of the walkway. There was space and there was light, even the 'blackboards' were yellow.

A fully carpeted suite of rooms at the front of the school intended for the headmistress and her staff were dismissed my Miss Welbank as too distant from the action and she took over a long narrow room next to the library. This room was very sparsely furnished with a desk opposite the door and any hapless girl summoned would knock and on the instruction 'Come!' would have to enter and walk the length of the room under the heady eye. Not a performance one would wish to repeat. My friend, who shall be nameless, was once so summoned on a Monday morning because she had been seen talking to a BOY in Village Street on the Saturday morning! And she wasn't even in school uniform at the time. It was a different world.

There was a sick bay run by Hilda Land who was amazingly gentle when I landed in it with a roaring appendix. Normally I was terrified of her. She was very strict about uniform and personal grooming. I remember she wanted shining heads for Speech Day as the visitors would be looking down on them from the gallery.

We had hockey practice 8 am sharp on the top pitch. Frost on the air and 'don't get picked for the team against Ockbrook Moravians they'll slaughter us they're so BIG!' Matches were played on Saturday mornings against visiting teams and there was great rivalry between the schools.

I can only remember one careers lecture and we were told we could either become nurses or teachers. One brave soul stood up and said she wanted to be an engineer. The lecturer thought she was being facetious and put her down in no uncertain manner.

Painting by Dame Laura Knight.
Ruby Loftus screwing a Breech-ring, 1943
Image Source: Wikipedia

Olive (née Naden) Allen

1938 Homelands such a long time ago and yet many times a flash back of names, faces and events come to mind.

We had one year of normal school routine, privileged girls in a brand new modern building, my previous schooling was at army schools as my father was a regular soldier.

Memories of the bag of shoes on our first day, the labelled clothes, those awful hats worn at every angle, skirts 5" above the knees when kneeling – much to my father's horror! The joy of a science lab with experiments, fantastic gym (which I hated) and lots of outside activities.

Photograph courtesy of Derby Evening Telegraph

Come that day in September 1939 and our world turned upside down, barrage balloons and airmen on the front lawn, blacked-out windows, air raid shelter practice; a siren sound, which still gives me a funny feeling all these years on.

Happy memories of the days at Mammerton Farm gathering in the harvest, picnic lunch in the fields. (I loved swapping Sybil's vegetarian sandwiches!) Eating the damsons off the trees as we worked. Packing up army parcels was another worthwhile task.

We were expected to work hard, but I look back with fondness on my years at Homelands, we were lucky to have this start in life.

Jacqueline (née Ashmole) Weston

I believe I am the only surviving member of my year; and I have very little to tell. I cannot remember ever having to go to the air raid shelter. I do remember the solemnity of the laying of the foundation stone by councillor Mrs Petty, the Lady Mayoress. I think only the sixth form were invited.

I remember the disappointment of Miss Welbank considering the sixth form study (a beautiful room at the front of the building on the first floor overlooking the drive) being too remote from the rest of the building so she denoted a stock-room in the middle of the classroom block on the first floor – we rarely used it, mind you she herself used a stock-room for when she took A-level history and signing points etc. – her secretary had quite a trek to find her when the phone went etc.

It was lovely not having to trek to playing fields and to have facilities for coaching tennis on the doorstep and to have sports day on our own grounds. Likewise Speech Day in our own school – not having to trek to the Central Hall. We thought the new dining room wonderful, and the covered way to it.

As for cookery, only a year at the most, and I believe that was shared with laundry – where we learnt about; blue bags, how to make starch, rinsing, boiling, mangling, dolly tubs and dolly pegs, I don't remember where the clothes were dried but I do remember having a practical test in ironing.

I shall always remember and be grateful for the good grounding I received in needlework classes. Everything we made we learnt a new skill – shoe bags – seams and chain stitch (our names) needlework wrappers (stitching on of tapes) and needlework aprons (binding with cross way pieces, even the pin cushion (button holes with a ribbon threaded through for decoration) our cookery aprons and hats (blue check with a cross stitch trim) and so on. The last thing I made was a dressing gown for college. I wonder how many of us wore the camisoles we made (exercise in adding lace)? So different to the textile and nutrition courses of today and of course laundry courses are no longer necessary with the invention of the automatic washers.

Dorothy (née Kent) Coulson

I can remember my first day at Homelands clearly. Dressed in blue and beige tobralco dress, with a panama hat and squeaky black shoes. I wore my uniform with pride.

Miss Moore was my class teacher, she had a formidable appearance with her grey hair and sausage curls, but actually had a gentle nature. Her boring scripture lessons twice a week from 2.40 to 3.20 pm almost put me off God for life, but her English lessons installed in me a love of English literature and an appreciation of English language.

Miss Bennett was a gentle French teacher and I coasted along in her classes, then in later years, the dreaded Miss Yates took over for French education and completely terrified me. As a result of my fear, I did my French homework to perfection and eventually gained a distinction in the matric examinations.

Miss Hilda Land was our burley gym teacher. Her sister Vera taught English for a few years whilst I was there.

I well remember many of the pupil's names, Meta Bull, Vera Seago, Sybil Ottewell, Patience Storer, Kathleen Hutt, Marion Compton and Margaret Platt. The pianists who took turns playing for morning hymns were Margaret Pitt and Vida Hand, The best swimmers one year were Joan Smith and Vivienne Keanan. In Form 1 in 1938 there was a quiet, clever girl called Lise Singer with long dark plats. I often think she must have been a Jewish refugee. Then there was Christine Prince with flaming red hair, Pattie and Celia Hullah and Joyce Bezant. A close friend of mine here in South Africa is Jean Lovemore, formerly Bolton. She and her sister Eileen were both at Homelands and both live in Port Elizabeth.

I was Dorothy Kent, the smallest girl in the school and remained the smallest until two years later when my younger sister Betty came to Homelands, and I have an older sister Joyce. Our claim to fame was that the three Kent sisters were all at Homelands together for a few years, we were in Darwin House.

Barbara (née Carr) Becker

How we all detested showers! Still today I will <u>not</u> take a shower. Americans can't understand me.

Veronica (née Tibbert) Kelly

In 1938 I had been a 'Hastings Street Bucketbanger' for a year, so that I started Homelands in the second form (I never did find out where the term 'bucketbanger' originated!).

The splendour of a school with an assembly hall which didn't also serve as a gym, a wonderful art room, laboratories and the novelty of yellow 'blackboards' with blue chalk was a great contrast to the Hastings Street School.

However, as one of the less academic students I chose to take Domestic Science and because the upstairs cookery room in Homelands House was not immediately ready the classes were held in a dungeon like cookery department in St James Road School – just around the comer from Hastings Street.

Reminiscent of the kitchens of a stately home, it had high windows you couldn't see out of, well scrubbed deal tables and an atmosphere of gloom. I spent one whole afternoon session learning how to make stewed apple and custard. I also learned how to clean silver with bath brick and to scrub tables using disgusting soft soap kept in a large jam pot.

The move to Homelands House was like a leap from the nineteenth to twentieth century, overnight, with modern cookers and a view of the Leicestershire Hills. Incidentally, I still make Miss McPherson's Scotch Apple Crumble!

Gina (née Smith) Kettlewell

I received a bicycle for gaining a scholarship, which seemed an encouraging start. This and the school bus became means of transport and, as Gina Smith, I joined our pristine new school in 1938 in form 1A, clutching a large collection of shoes. The latter required for indoor, outdoor gym, games and tennis. All necessary to help preserve the magnificent oak blocked floors and special gymnasium floor. They were housed in a shoe bag, which eventually evolved from the needlework class, made in navy material and emblazoned with name embroidered in red and hung along with coats and hats in strict numbered rotation in the cloakroom.

Air-raid drill, gas masks, dried egg, tennis on the lawn, hockey team, sewing outsize bloomers, homework record and Miss Whitt's House plays performed on the stage, spring to mind with uncanny clarity. As does the wrath of Miss Welbank when her rigid path was not pursued.

A queue of people waiting to be issued with gas masks outside Normanton School, on Village Street in 1938

Photograph courtesy of Normanton-by-Derby Local History Group

I soon learned that house points were not easily gained. Two consecutive good marks equalling one point. This involved queuing outside Miss Welbank's office door in fear and trepidation to gain her signature thus proving it valid. Whereas losing some proved comparatively easy, i.e. pushing cycle up centre drive (banned to pupils), not wearing hat firmly on one's head, running or straying from the right-hand side of the corridors and coughing in Miss Yate's French lesson. The latter usually ensured in writing large amounts of French prose.

Painting with Miss Adnams in the superb bright new art room was a joy indeed, and a reminder of colours gained for Arts and Crafts. These were distributed on annual Prize day when parents of recipients were allowed a seat in the main hall gallery. We would all be resplendent in strict crisp uniform and our graduate unmarried mistresses duly robed.

Miss Marion Adnams

Photograph courtesy of John V. Rooks

Each new term saw strict new rules adhered to. We obediently knelt on the floor whilst the hem of our tunic was measured, ensuring it was the regulation length of five inches above the knee. A truly astonishing sight as we all flourished and grew taller, and in some cases wider, pushing our tunic pleats to their limits. Add navy knickers, with pocket, lisle stockings and suspenders, striped tie with white blouse, and royal blue girdle for hockey team. We were a great advert for the famous St. Trinian girls.

At the onset of war in 1939 we carried a gas mask at all times and inspections were required. This involved each of us wearing our mask whilst the form mistress tested the front breathing nozzle with a piece of card; as we breathed in, the card remaining in place confirmed we were still breathing.

Air-raid drill was another essential. We sat on planks of wood in large Anderson shelters hastily dug in the playing fields. A small partition at one end was curtained off and contained a bucket. A pupil's hand was raised, the form mistress nodded, and the girl went behind the curtain. The mistress then raised her hands as in conducting mode, head poised, and said, 'Now girls, ready, one, two, three' and we all burst forth with 'O Lass of Richmond Hill' with hearty gusto.

On one occasion, an apparition appeared at the entrance to our shelter draped from head to foot in gas protective gear, complete with long breathing pipe coiling from the face mask, a truly amazing sight. Even more so when Miss Welbank's voice echoed from its depths; instructing her Gels to sit up straight and keep minds focused on the next lesson.

Bombs demolished some houses nearby resulting in our school water supply becoming disconnected, resulting in a day's holiday, with homework of course.

Bomb crater in Derby Lane, Normanton, after the air raid of January 1941. Derby's heaviest bombing during the war

Photograph courtesy of Normanton-by-Derby Local History Group

Derby Lane – December 2016. Image courtesy of K. S. Dhindsa © 2016

We laboriously sewed enormous bloomers in the needlework class, not sure why. We designed our own pincushion, needlecase, shoe bag, cookery apron, and sewing apron. Learned how to hem, dam and pattern make. We also learned how to carefully iron the hem of a delicate handkerchief and cook with dried egg in the domestic science room above the large dining area in the old house across the quadrangle and covered walk from the school.

Homework, of which there was a great deal, had to be recorded in a special book which in turn was checked and signed by a staff. Only certain time was allowed for each subject, needless to say the records were seldom an accurate account of time spent. For the fourth year girls were allowed, on occasions, the peaceful sanctuary of the library for extra special study.

Throughout the school, exams were taken each term and progress carefully monitored with appropriate up and down gradings. The emphasis was always to work harder. In retrospect the curriculum was excellent. At 10 and a half to 11 years of age it probably appeared daunting.

Fitness was a prime factor. Daily physical education and shower, hockey, netball, rounders, and tennis on the lawn proved enjoyable for the energetic type, the less keen would be in awe of 'Hilda'. All this plus food rationing dispelled any ideas of being overweight, and Miss Hilda Land ruled her gymnasium and games empire with a rod of iron. For swimming, also part of her domain, we repaired to Reginald Street Baths where it was advisable to keep afloat at all times and appear to be swimming.

Reginald Street Swimming Baths, 1981

Photograph courtesy of Derby Evening Telegraph

Science could be fun; perched high on stools in the well equipped laboratory, surrounded by Bunsen burners, busily dissecting worms, stretched out and pinned to a bed of wax, and wondering what might happen next as Miss Steel waved a pair of lungs about with great flourish.

Music and dancing lessons were taken. The latter included country and ballroom. An annual ball was arranged in the main hall and each pupil made a programme to be filled by potential partners, all members of the school. The opposite sex, were never allowed over the threshold, so tall girls were required to learn lead steps.

It was a fascinating learning curve, one I am sure we all look back upon with great nostalgia.

Sybil (née Ottewell) Brant

Ward shoes, highly polished corridors, Rose beds at the front and later dug up for the barrage balloon. Air-raid shelters at the back and growing flowers and vegetables there. The smell of paraldehyde in the science lab and pinning worms in wax below. Liberty vests, woollen stockings, doing P.T. in vests and navy knickers. Cookery classes and taking stew home in a bowl in a basket the smell still lingering in the cookery room the next day.

The smell of the gas masks when we had 'drill'. P.T., Swimming, Art, English, Geography were my favourite subjects, and I liked all the teachers.

I was very happy during those years, in spite of the noise of the German bombers going overhead at night and the stray bomb falling and causing such devastation.

Beryl (née Tinkler) Holland

I went flax picking somewhere, if I remember correctly in the Stenson area.

I did go watercolour painting with Miss Adnams – quite a few times – and I have the 'pictures' to prove it. (Not on show I might add!) I quite liked her and seem to think that as a result I was expected to sit in the front seat whilst she was driving, those who weren't so keen sat further away.

I have always thought that the hymns that would be sung at assembly, the numbers of which were already shown on the board, would be changed if the sirens had gone the night before – and we therefore could not sing; 'Ye that have spent the silent night in sleep and quiet rest'. Not surprising really.

Jean (née Dallison) Mozley

Bert and Jean Mozley on their wedding day

Photograph courtesy of Jean Mozley

As a 90-year-old maybe I am one of the oldest 'Old Girls' from Homelands Grammar School. I went there when it was first built. Prior to that we were in Hastings Street at the Central School.

Homelands was a beautiful School. Our Headmistress was Miss Welbank and she put the fear of death into all her girls. I remember the names of some of the teachers. Miss Lloydall was my first teacher. She took French. My favourite was Miss Adnams – (Art) with Miss Vera Land (English) a close second. There was a Miss Brooks who tried to teach us how to sew. I did not like sewing at all but have thanked Miss Brooks so many times since. She was very strict and we had to have perfect samples of our work. I can't remember how many times I had to unpick my stitches but after I married and had two daughters – I was able to make all their outfits – thanks to dear Miss Brooks. Miss Witt and Miss Peyton both taught Maths. I liked them both. Miss Yates taught French and taught singing. She was very strict and not too well liked. I think we were all relieved when Miss Yates retired and our new teacher took over. She was young and very nice.

I left school just after the war started and worked at Rolls-Royce. I lost touch with most of my classmates. In 1955 my husband and I moved to Canada with our two daughters. I have since managed to find two ex Homeland friends who were not in my class but who also live in Canada. (Sadly 3,000 miles from Victoria where I live – so haven't been able to meet them). However – we are in touch on the Internet all the time.

Jean Mozley, 12th December 2015. Victoria, BC, Canada.

Homelands mistress inspired love of art

Recent memories of Homelands School in the 1940s have prompted Jean Mozley to send the following missive all the way from Canada.

Jean, wife of former Derby County and England right back Bert Mozley, still likes to keep in touch with her roots across the water.

She writes: 'My love of art stems from the wonderful instructions that art mistress Marion Adnams brought into our classroom at Homelands School every week.

'I was a pupil there and she was our form mistress in 1940. She was my favourite teacher and I have so much to thank her for. I am still painting watercolours at the age of 83 and loving every minute.

'I think of Miss Adnams often. She was a gem.'

Jean Mozley, 6th October 2008. Derby Telegraph

I am a great lover of animals and always enjoyed trying to draw and later to paint anything on four legs! Miss Adnams always encouraged me but she could get very angry if something was 'not done in the way that she had specified'. I remember having to do one assignment twice, (and I was very 'miffed' – I thought my first effort was much better than the second one, which Miss Adnams preferred). (The nerve of an eleven year old!) I haven't painted now for quite some time but enjoyed many years with my watercolours thanks to my old Homelands teacher. God Bless you Miss Adnams!

Jean Mozley, 9th January 2017, Victoria, BC, Canada.

I'm NOT having a bath

Watercolour – Jean Mozley

Marion Elizabeth Adnams

3rd December 1898 – 24th October 1995

Photograph courtesy of John V. Rooks

An accomplished surrealist painter whose artistic development began late. After Parkfields Cedars School, Derby, she wished to study art but was encouraged to attend University College, Nottingham, where she obtained a BA in Modern Languages in 1919. She first studied art part-time in life classes at Derby School of Art in 1930, one year after the surrealist painter Alfred Bladen (q.v.) assumed the position of Head of Drawing. Although teaching modern languages full-time at Homelands Grammar School for Girls, Derby, Adnams undertook more painting with a view to an art teacher's diploma, which she gained in 1938. Her work attracted attention locally and by 1939 was being taken up by London galleries. Adnams was also influenced by Magritte and Paul Nash, but claimed that the contemplative character of much of her work sprang from her religious belief. She painted with clarity and conviction, often depicting natural forms or small animals displaced from their familiar contexts. In 1946 she assumed the post of senior lecturer and head of department at Derby Training College. Adnams was noted for her self-assurance and strong personality, often making her difficult to deal with. Longevity ensured she was known to a wide circle of people. Retiral from her final post as Head of Art, Derby Diocesan College of Education, came in 1960. Work of that decade was strongly influenced by the life and landscape of Provence where she had chosen to live. For 30 years, from the late 1930s, she showed continuously in London. She later resumed living in Otter Street, in the small house where she was born and had lived most of her life. She died there, aged ninety-six.

Exhibited: London from *c.* 1939; RBSA; Midland Group, Nottingham; Midland Group Gallery, Nottingham, retro. 1971; Immanuel Church, Stapenhill; Burton on Trent, murals 1964–5.

Examples: Manchester AG; Salford AG; Leicester AG; Wolverhampton AG; Derby AG; Nottingham Castle AG.

The aforementioned artist profile is courtesy of *Who's Who of Artists in Derbyshire* by John Fineran.

Alter Ego
Mary Elizabeth Adnams

Derby Museum and Art Gallery

Alter Ego, by Marion Adnams, oil on board, 1945
(Derby Museums Trust)
Image Source: Wikipedia

Presented to the Gallery by Homelands Grammar School for Girls, Headmistress,
Dorothea Susannah Gilbert.

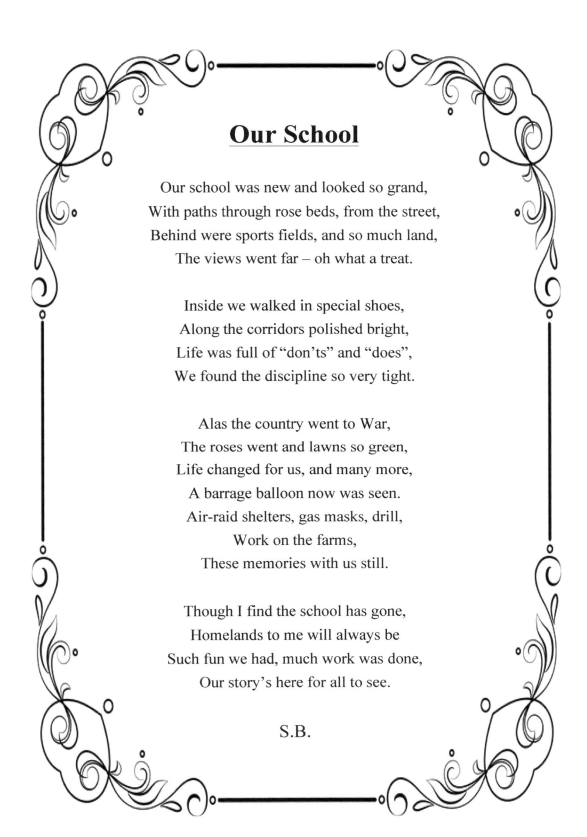

Our School

Our school was new and looked so grand,
With paths through rose beds, from the street,
Behind were sports fields, and so much land,
The views went far – oh what a treat.

Inside we walked in special shoes,
Along the corridors polished bright,
Life was full of "don'ts" and "does",
We found the discipline so very tight.

Alas the country went to War,
The roses went and lawns so green,
Life changed for us, and many more,
A barrage balloon now was seen.
Air-raid shelters, gas masks, drill,
Work on the farms,
These memories with us still.

Though I find the school has gone,
Homelands to me will always be
Such fun we had, much work was done,
Our story's here for all to see.

S.B.

MARJORIE'S MISCELLANY – Part I

Marjorie Calow

The Staff

'A good gymnast always sits up straight.' These words put the fear of God into me. The year was 1942 and I was an ugly, smelly, fat ten-year-old – so fat that I had to have extra clothing coupons because my regulation gym slip had to be made specially, since none was available in the shops to fit me. The speaker was Miss Hilda Land and it was my first day at Homelands Grammar School for Girls. We were in the dining room of Homelands House, which was separated from the main building by a covered way, and Miss Land was on dinner duty. The rest of the staff sat at tables in the two bay windows. I was at a table seating – as I remember it perhaps sixteen girls, with other first-formers. Miss Land was patrolling the whole dining room, a large room which accommodated all the girls who stayed for school dinners. (Of the dinners I remember very little, except that we were frequently served one-inch cubes of stringy swede, which put me off that vegetable for life.) She must have picked on me because I was slouching and because I was manifestly not gymnast material. Throughout my time at Homelands, gym and games lessons were torture for me. I loathed the idea of stripping down to my vest and navy knickers and somehow I always managed to dodge the communal showers. Moreover, I was terrified of vaulting over the horse, climbing the ropes or climbing the wall bars. Somehow I succeeded in getting out of all these ghastly activities, although I didn't mind the physical jerks with which the gym lesson started. As for games: netball, hockey and rounders all filled me with equal horror. In the fullness of time Miss Land and I established a modus vivendi. I simply can't remember exactly how this was negotiated, but I think it was a combination of me hiding (I've no idea where) at the relevant times and Miss Land deciding that the best way of coping with me was to pretend that I didn't exist. However, to this day I can still see, in my mind's eye, her terrifying figure: she was always dressed in a gymslip and wore Plimsolls. For the record, it is only fair to say that I now believe that her bark was <u>far</u> worse than her bite. The poor lady died young and very suddenly of a heart attack (I think after I left school).

There were two other staff members who terrified me, albeit to afar lesser extent than Miss Land did. The classrooms opened off two corridors, one on the ground floor and one above it on the first floor. Miss Yates patrolled the top corridor. She taught French, although she never taught me, and seemed, to my youthful eyes, to be <u>ancient</u>. With hindsight, I suppose she must have been approaching sixty, since she had gone when I returned later as a teacher. She had grey hair drawn back into a bun and wore long dresses. Between lessons, we were supposed to walk demurely, in single file, between classrooms, without jostling each other or stepping out of line. If any girl offended, Miss Yates would fix her with an icy glare and beckon her silently, using the forefinger of her right hand. Punishment – I think in the form of lines to be written out after school – would then be meted out.

Miss Welbank, the headmistress, was the other person who terrified me. She appeared to be of the same vintage as Miss Yates, was of a similar build and had a similar taste in clothes. Her dresses were brown (those of Miss Yates were grey) and she wore her hair in a similar tight, grey bun. She occupied a room on one of the shorter corridors linking the long classroom corridors with the front of the building. On the rare occasions when she left her lair, her very appearance would strike terror into our hearts.

On the subject of headmistresses, the successor to Miss Welbank was Miss Gilbert. She was a horse of a very different colour. Her appearance was that of a 'modern' woman: her hair was cut in a bob and she wore smart suits. Prior to her stint at Homelands, she had been at Cheltenham Ladies College. However, her attempts to transform us down-to-earth Derbyshire girls into clones of Cheltenham ladies were not popular. In actual fact, all I can remember of these attempts was the diktat that we should wear blouses under our sweaters (not such an outrageous idea, with hindsight). The length of time she stayed with us is not clear in my memory, but I think it was only about a couple of years. She was followed by Miss Helmore. I remember her as quite an attractive woman (perhaps in her mid-forties), with white hair, delicate hands and a definite presence. Every morning we had Assembly in the hall and I can still see her sweeping onto the platform to take Assembly; she wore her academic gown, of course, as did all the staff. Until her fairly dramatic appearance, a senior girl would play 'classical' music (part of a Beethoven sonata, or some such) on the piano, fading out the music at the moment Miss Helmore appeared. I have a clear recollection of my annoyance at the music being curtailed in this way. Later, when I was a member of staff, I learned that Miss Helmore was not fond of music and that the music mistress, Miss Newman, was often disappointed at the Head's lack of appreciation of her efforts (for instance, in training the school choir). Whether it was Miss Gilbert or Miss Helmore who changed the location of the Headmistress's office, I am not sure, but certainly by Miss Helmore's time she was ensconced in an office at the front of the building. The sequence of rooms at the front (looking from right to left facing the school) was: the headmistress's study, the secretary's office, front door, waiting room, staff room and staff cloakroom. Set back at each end were cloakrooms and lavatories for the girls. The secretary, from 1942 to 1950, was Miss Orton, who in appearance and dress was very like Miss Welbank. She guarded Miss Helmore with her honour, but I subsequently learned she was seen by some to be a difficult colleague.

My feelings about Miss Helmore were mixed. In many ways I admired and respected her. However, in 1948, the trendy development in girls' grammar schools was to have a science sixth form. My School Certificate results were good in all subjects, but, on the basis of my Distinction in general science and Credit in mathematics, Miss Helmore decided that I, together with another girl called Vera Seago, should be in her science sixth. Although I colluded with this decision I at least had the sense to resist being pushed into medicine. With hindsight, it is perfectly obvious that I should have done English; my School Certificate result for that subject was also a Distinction, but it was to be another forty years before I obtained a degree in English. The English teacher, Miss Witt, put up a good fight on my behalf, but in vain. As a consolation prize, she was allowed to take me for one lesson a week and would set me essays on subjects such as: is anticipation better than realisation?

I wonder if she had read *Les Liaisons Dangereuses* by Laclos? Probably she had, since she gave the appearance of being worldly wise (she was a devout Catholic …). She had white hair, dressed in a bun, was rotund and had a lovely smile and a wicked sense of humour. (I corresponded with her until her death.) One day, when we were in the fourth or fifth form, there was a flu epidemic and the class was much reduced. She swept into the classroom as was her wont (she once gave us, as an example of a simile, the sentence: 'Miss Witt entered the classroom like a ship in full sail') and greeted us with: 'Good Morning, half-class', as we rose to our feet. To which one wag audibly replied: 'Good Morning, half-Witt.' Needless to say, she was promptly forgiven once the merriment had subsided. Miss Witt was the first person to make me realise that a Shakespearean text could be interpreted in a variety of ways. One of our set books for School Certificate English was Macbeth. In Act I, Scene vii (lines 58 and 59), the conversation between Macbeth and Lady Macbeth includes the lines:

Macbeth: If we should fail, -
Lady Macbeth: We fail!

Miss Witt pointed out that the words 'We fail!' could be delivered either as an incredulous interrogation or with a shrug of resignation.

My first form mistress was Miss Moore. She was tall and thin, with a pasty-white face and hair cut in a bob with a curious halt-fringe. My recollection (but surely this can't be right?) was that she spent the first lesson with us describing how the Egyptians prepared a body for mummification. As a squeamish ten-year-old, I was horrified by the description of how the internal organs were removed and placed in a jar. This must be an example of false memory syndrome but why is my recollection so clear?

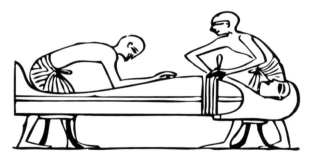

Whatever the truth, I remember Miss Moore as a pleasant form-mistress with a sense of humour. I believe she had a penchant for foreign travel. Our classroom was at one end of the upstairs corridor, looking out onto the mature trees in the grounds of the school.

Some of us had a crush on a young Mathematics teacher called Miss Haworth. We called her 'Fopey' because she pronounced 'three and fourpence' as 'three and fo pence'. Miss Pakeman (old and going bald) also taught Mathematics. Was she the one we called 'Juicy' because of her habit of ending every explanation with 'D'you see?' Perhaps that was a different Mathematics teacher .... My memory is much clearer about Mrs Blaine. She was young and pale, with a sad expression. Her married status (most unusual amongst teachers in those days) stimulated our young imaginations.

Our fantasy was that her husband was away at the war and she was sad because she was pining for him. (I believe there was some truth in the first part of this speculation, but, although she might well have been pining for him, a fantasy later circulated to the effect that he was finding consolation elsewhere.)

Another married member of staff was an art mistress called Mrs Carr, who was older and jollier. The other art mistress was Marion Adnams, who was in fact a surrealist artist of some merit, and was sufficiently distinguished to merit an exhibition devoted to her work some time after she retired from teaching. She lived to a ripe old age and, although she was blind towards the end of her life, still enjoyed the attentions of a number of adoring young men. Somehow, by some process of intuition, I always suspected that she had a – shall we say interesting – private life. Not that I ever had much contact with her. The art room was the only room on the opposite side of the upstairs corridor to the classrooms. Like the rest of the building, it was thoughtfully designed, with sky lights to give maximum north light. Although I remember the room well, I don't remember what I did in it. What happened, I think, was that, like Miss Land (and, for that matter, the Needlework mistress), Miss Adnams decided that the only way to handle such an intractable pupil was simply to ignore her.

Mrs Wignall was another jolly married lady, considerably younger than Mrs Carr. Her husband, unlike Mr Carr, occasionally put in an appearance to help with school plays. History was Mrs Wignall's subject. My main memory is of her pacing backwards and forwards in front of the class, spitting out the names of Prime Ministers, which we were expected to memorise. Although I achieved a Distinction in School Certificate, none of the history I learned has stayed with me, much to my regret. Another subject that really was not for me was Domestic Science. For our weekly lesson, we had to take in a basket of ingredients. I have absolutely no memory of any culinary delights that I presumably produced, but I do remember getting an excellent mark for an essay on 'How to Wash Up'. The secret, as I recollect, is to start with the cutlery, progress through crockery in various stages of greasiness and finish with the saucepans. We were taught by Miss Leishman, a very tall, elegant lady with a posh accent, who was probably in her thirties. (Miss Coulson was around at some stage, but whether she preceded or succeeded Miss Leishman I don't remember.) The domestic science room, again specially designed for the purpose, was in Homelands House, above the dining room. Miss Leishman occupied a flat in the same building, but I've no idea why she was the only resident member of staff, since she was in no sense a Matron (we didn't have a Matron).

When the dining room was not being used for eating it was the location for music lessons (the piano occupied a position near the bay window where the staff took their meals). Miss Rhoda Newman was the music teacher. She was a talented pianist, who played in public for local choirs and the like. Her job was to try to teach us music appreciation (a fairly thankless task as far as most of the girls were concerned) and to train us to perform the songs we would sing on Speech Day. She also trained the school choir, but I was not a member of this. Every so often she would be seized by a bout of uncontrollable coughing, which would last for several minutes; I never found out the cause of this.

Her temper was unpredictable. Once she raged at us as philistines (I don't think she actually used that word) because we sniggered – I've no idea why – at having to sing 'Orpheus with his lute'. Her taste in clothes was a bit strange; she favoured cardigans covered with multi-coloured bobbles. She suffered more than we realised, I think, at Miss Helmore's lack of appreciation of her efforts. Although she lived, apparently contentedly, with her aged mother, I sometimes wondered if she had hidden depths.

When I returned to Homelands to teach, I had an intriguing conversation with her in the staff cloakroom one Friday. She commented that I looked happy and I said the reason for this was that I would be spending the weekend with my husband (I was newly married and he was doing his National Service). Her response to this was: 'But how much more exciting it would be if you were going to spend the weekend with someone else's husband'. Ho, hum! There was another Miss Newman who came in to teach music on a part-time basis. She was a large woman with a florid complexion and was rather strange; I preferred 'our' Miss Newman.

Our form-mistress at one stage (when we were in the fourth form?) and later our sixth-form mistress was Miss Graham. She was a brilliant mathematician who had worked at the prestigious Manchester Grammar School. I adored her, although she was a strict disciplinarian. On one occasion a dozy pupil was obviously not paying attention. Miss Graham commented: 'You know, there was once someone who said "Sometimes I sits and thinks, and then again I just sits" I think you just sits.'

One aspect of Miss Graham's character that fascinated me was the fact that she was a Baptist lay preacher. I was brought up as a strict Baptist and when I heard she was going to preach at Ticknall I went to hear her. (No, I can't remember anything about her sermon.) Later she became an Anglican, but my father always had a soft spot for her, partly because of the Baptist connection and partly because of her lovely personality. As a sixth-form mistress her support for me when my mother had a nervous breakdown in the middle of my Higher School Certificate was something I shall never forget.

Homelands Sports Day, 1955. Seated teachers are from left to right: Miss Drinkwater (Maths), Miss Graham (Maths) and Miss Robinson (French)

Photograph courtesy of Marjorie Calow

On the day that Miss Graham joined the staff, in September 1946, another new member of staff also arrived. This was Miss Robinson. She and Miss Graham rapidly formed a close friendship that lasted for the rest of their lives. Miss Robinson taught French. When I knew her later as a friend she alleged that Joyce Mercer and I used to sit at the back of the room scowling. Of this I have no recollection. What I do recall, with considerable pleasure, is that she taught us to sing songs in French (she had a good voice). She also told us the story of Miss Moberley and Miss Jordain (alias Elizabeth Morison and Frances Lamont) and their strange encounter with the ghosts at Versailles. Some girls found Miss Robinson too strict for their taste; she did have a sarcastic tongue. However, I got on fine with her. Moreover, she had a sense of humour. She told me later, when I went back as a teacher, that she once kept a particularly obnoxious pupil in after school and started the proceedings with the statement: 'I've toughed cracker nuts than you', whereupon both teacher and pupil collapsed in a fit of giggles.

Because I specialised in science, I got to know the science staff well when I was in the sixth form. Before that, I think in the fourth form, we were taught chemistry by Miss Steel, a pleasant, gentle woman with a Scots accent. She was replaced by Miss Neale. While we were still in the junior forms, we were pretty cruel to Miss Neale. She was a short lady, spherical in shape, with apple cheeks and cropped grey hair. Once she informed us that women of her generation hadn't married because all the young men had been killed in the First World War. This statement was greeted with derision: how could anyone possibly fancy her? In the sixth form I was taught by her for much of the time, since my subjects were chemistry, physics and pure mathematics. She left at the time I got my chemistry degree (in 1953) and, at Miss Helmore's invitation, I replaced her. I shall say more about this (with hindsight) somewhat mind-boggling event in the second part of this narrative. Miss Neale and I corresponded regularly until her death. I had visited her home in White Street in Derby while I was in the sixth form and later, after returning to Homelands, visited her in Faversham. The memory of what she told me about her time at Homelands has faded, but the impression remains that she was not happy there, perhaps due to a personality clash with Miss Helmore.

Miss Elliott taught biology. She was short, with a grey bun and a puffed-out but at the same time flat chest, giving her something of the appearance of a penguin. Whereas the chemistry laboratory was on the side corridor leading from the main corridor to the front of the building, the Biology laboratory was on the main corridor. I mention this because I have a particularly vivid memory concerning the preparation room next to the main laboratory. Because I was supposed to be specialising in chemistry, but had done only School Certificate general science, I had to do physics-with-chemistry at School Certificate level in my first year in the sixth form. My memory is hazy, but there must have been some suggestion that I should do biology for Higher School Certificate. The long corridor faced south and I spent one hot summer afternoon alone in the preparation room with a rabbit that I was supposed to be dissecting (having moved on from earthworms, frogs and dogfish). The heat and the stench of formaldehyde were too much for me: at that point I decided that I did not want to do biology. Nevertheless, I have fond memories of Miss Elliott as a colleague.

One Whitsuntide we travelled to Grimsby together (my husband's parents lived in Grimsby) in her little sit-up-and-beg Austin Seven. It was a pleasant journey, involving a picnic in a bluebell wood at one point (or did I dream this?).

Having made the decision to do physics rather than biology (and I have no recollection of any hassle over this decision) I had to be taught. A Mr Swift had visited to teach physics at some stage, but I've no idea what happened to him.

In any case, I (and presumably Vera, although I don't remember this) was sent to the art school in Green Lane to be taught by Mr Price. He was, as I recall, a pleasant, quite good-looking, middle-aged man. Inevitably, since I'd hardly clapped eyes on a man outside my immediate family circle before then, I developed a mild crush on him. He handled the situation with tact and, since I worked hard to please him, I duly got a Credit for Physics in my Higher School Certificate. (For the record, I also got a Credit for Chemistry and a Pass in Pure Mathematics. These results were sufficient for me to secure a place at Queen Mary College, University of London, to study for a BSc Special Chemistry degree – which I eventually got by the skin of my teeth.)

QUEEN MARY COLLEGE

(UNIVERSITY OF LONDON).

Please address to
THE SECRETARY

Ministry's ref: RP/EC/8847
CALOW, Marjorie Elizabeth

MINISTRY OF EDUCATION,
(Teachers Branch),
36–38, Berkeley Square,
LONDON, W.1.

3 SEP 195?

TEL: GROSVENOR 6060 (for "Training" enquiries)
MAYFAIR 9400 (for "Qualifications" ")

Sir (or Madam),

1. With reference to your appointment as a teacher in Derby Homelands Grammar School, I am directed by the Minister of Education to inform you that, subject to the verification of your qualifications in accordance with E.R. Memorandum No. 101 by your employers, you are regarded as a qualified teacher under Regulation 11(2) of the Schools Grant Regulations 1951. This Regulation applies to maintained or assisted primary (including nursery) schools, or secondary (grammar, modern or technical) schools, and to those schools, other than direct grant grammar schools, which receive their grants direct from the Minister.

The Building

Saturday 8th September 1951

Photograph courtesy of Marjorie Calow

Homelands was a beautiful building, but some of us had to make a considerable journey to reach it. In the 1940s few families had cars and children were certainly not ferried to school.

Melbourne, where I lived, was eight miles away from Derby. The first leg of the journey involved a ride on a bus run by the Trent Motor Traction Company. We got off the bus at Allenton and had to run like mad to catch the double-decker 'special' bus provided by Derby Corporation. This dropped us at The Barracks and from there we walked to Homelands. The journey home after school was different. My memory is unreliable here. At one stage a Trent 'special', which also served Bemrose School (one of the two grammar schools for boys), stopped at Homelands en route to Melbourne. However, I think this was in the 1950s, when I returned to Homelands to teach. Certainly in my early years at the school we walked to the trolley bus (was it a trolley bus?) stop in Derby Lane. This took us to Babington Lane, in Derby. We walked through the slums (of which I have only a hazy memory) from The Spot to Cockpit Hill and thence to the bus station, where we boarded a Trent bus for Melbourne. Sometimes we would make a detour to the Central Educational shop in St Peter's Street, where I would browse amongst the books and, very occasionally, buy one. Once I had resolved to buy a slim volume on the Bayeux Tapestry, only to find the last copy had already been sold. To this very day I remember my intense feeling of disappointment. On other occasions I would walk along East Street and gaze longingly at coffrets of soap and talcum powder displayed in the window of a shop near the corner where the street joined The Morledge. Just occasionally, during the summer months, my parents would be waiting for me at the end of the school drive in their car. This was always a surprise treat and it was a tremendous thrill to look out of the cloakroom window and see that they were there. Part of the thrill was the feeling of superiority it gave me to be collected in a car. What few (if any) of my classmates realised was that the possession of a car did not indicate that we were a bit higher up the social scale than some of them. Quite the reverse, in fact. My father was a hard-working, hands-on, self-employed carpenter, joiner and undertaker and the black Austin 16 (registration number CTO 490) was a necessity for his business (he used it to transport coffins).

We had few holidays and those evening trips into the Derbyshire countryside were often the only breaks from work that my father had. (I was puzzled when Miss Hughes – another delightful English teacher who taught me for only a short time – once queried a comment I included in one of my essays to the effect that my father spent many evenings 'booking'. That was what making out bills and all the other jobs involved in running a business was called in our house – and I thought all fathers spent time 'booking'.)

After that digression on the journeys to and from school I now return to my recollections of the building. Having arrived at the gate, we got into the school by using one of the two side drives and entrances. The centre drive and main entrance were reserved for staff and visitors; there were no cars to clutter up the drives. It was assumed that we would treat our beautiful building with respect and this we did. In these graffiti-infested days it seems inconceivable that all the Christmas parties should be cancelled one year because a mark had appeared on a wall somewhere and no one would own up to doing the deed. (I believe in the end it was established that one girl was inadvertently responsible: a pencil protruding from her satchel made the mark as she walked along.) The cloakrooms were adjacent to the side entrances that we used. In the cloakroom we each had a peg on which to hang our shoe bag. As we entered the building, we changed from outdoor to indoor shoes. This rule was to protect the parquet floors in the corridors and classrooms. It is a rule of which I still thoroughly approve, although in the twenty-first century anyone trying to introduce such a rule would be branded a lunatic. Were the stairs at each end of the long corridor at the back of the building really made of marble? That is how I remember them, anyway. The back of the building faced south and the views from the classrooms (which were aligned along the corridors on the ground and first floors) were spectacular. Quite apart from the distant view over the Vale of Trent to Breedon-on-the-Hill, the view of the grounds themselves was magnificent. From the central entrance on the south side a path led, with grass and mature trees on both sides, to another path at right angles. Below this were playing fields, with the netball court on the right. Steps led down to another path and more playing fields. Beyond the entrance at the west end of the downstairs corridor was a covered way, leading to Homelands House. This building, as already mentioned, housed the kitchen, dining room and domestic science rooms; it must have been a spectacular building in the days when it was a private residence.

During the war, presumably under some loan scheme, prints of paintings were hung on the corridor walls of the main building. One that hung outside Miss Welbank's study was 'Wood on the Downs' by Paul Nash. I loved that picture and many years later was able to buy a print of it, which still hangs in my sitting-room. I also made a pilgrimage to London to see the original – which is in the Aberdeen Art Gallery – when it was on view during an exhibition of Nash's paintings at the Tate Gallery in 1975.

This caused me temporarily to become disenchanted by my puny little print, since the actual painting was much larger than I had realised, but now I love my print as much as when I bought it. This anecdote illustrates how even someone who was (and to some extent still is) an ignoramus where art is concerned, could, by a process of osmosis, absorb some appreciation of beauty. Another memory is of being taken to an exhibition of Dutch flower paintings; I still remember the sense of wonder they evoked. Concerning specific rooms in the building, I loved them all, apart from, for obvious reasons, the gymnasium and the sick bay (which was Miss Land's lair). I loved the very modern-seeming stacking chairs in the hall (what happened to them, I wonder?) and I loved all the furniture, much of which had been specially designed. In the prefects' room on the top corridor many fascinating adolescent discussions took place (how innocent and un-streetwise we were!). Of course, being a chemist, my most vivid memories are of the chemistry laboratory, including being taught by Miss Neale in the preparation room when in the sixth form (when there were only two pupils – so the teaching could almost be described as individual tuition), and later, as a teacher, doing demonstrations in the main laboratory, with no safety spectacles or indeed any of the paraphernalia with which current practical work is carried out.

With hindsight (I was only dimly aware of this at the time), what I find touching about this magnificent building was the vision of the city fathers (including female councillors ...) in providing it. Before Homelands (whose pupils from the second form upwards, and some of the staff, came from the Central School for Girls) there had been only one grammar school for girls in the borough, this was Parkfields Cedars. Homelands was a worthy rival (and there <u>was</u> rivalry between the two establishments), not least because the purpose-built building provided an environment that was conducive to study (I have, of course, already described the other element in its success, namely the dedicated staff).

Such is the depth of the affection that I feel for the Homelands I knew, that tears frequently come into my eyes when I think of how the building (<u>and</u> the vision) has been debased since the rot set in (in the 1960s). Now, in 2002, its very future is in doubt.

What a contrast there is between the behaviour of the city fathers today and those of the 1930s. Derby was fortunate to have, as its Borough Architect in the 1930s, Mr C. H. Aslin.

The vandals are indeed at the gate when treasures such as Homelands School and the bus station (which he also designed) are under threat. Call me a dinosaur, but to me such so-called planning is lunacy.

64

Evening Telegraph

FRIDAY, OCTOBER 13, 2000   29p   CITY FINAL EDITION

Inquiry into R-R blaze: See Page 3

BETRAYED

Huge deal for A3XX engines

ROLLS-ROYCE this afternoon announced that it had won a £1.02bn order to supply engines for the Airbus A3XX superjumbo.

Singapore Airlines has chosen the Trent 900 to power its new fleet of up to 25 aircraft.

The order is the largest that the Derby company has won for several months.

Singapore has long been a strong customer of Rolls in preference to competitors Pratt & Whitney and General Electric.

The decision means that the Trent 900, which is still under development, will be the lead engine for the A3XX.

It will be the sole powerplant for initial production of the European-built superjumbo.

John Cheffins, president of Civil Aerospace Rolls-Royce, said: "The excellent in-service record of the Trent 800 on Boeing 777s was an important factor in this decision."

THE people who control Derby's schools need to take some lessons in democracy.

That is the view of the hundreds of parents and residents who object to the decision by Derby City Council to close one of the city's oldest secondary schools.

Village Community School in Normanton seems destined to be killed off as the council attempts to deal with more than 2,000 surplus pupil places in Derby.

The authority has decided that, from September of next year, Village's 500 pupils will be divided between two other schools with surplus places – Bemrose and Sin-

Telegraph COMMENT

fin Community Schools.

Those who have protested at the closure decision feel betrayed by the system of public "consultation" that led to the school's demise and by the fact that their views were swept aside by the people who carried out the consultation.

They feel betrayed because they cannot turn to the councillors they elected – council leader Robert Jones and his deputy Chris Williamson – because they are among the decision-makers who have signed Village Community

School's death warrant.

In short, although they have formed a Save Our School action group, the protesters feel powerless in their desire to urge the council to rethink its strategy and look for ways to keep open this vital education link in what is already a socially-deprived community.

Which is why, today, the Derby Evening Telegraph is speaking up for the 1,500 people who have protested at the closure and feel that the council has not listened to their views.

On their behalf, we ask the council some basic questions about its decision.

No-one is underestimating the problems at Village Community School. But after years of decline and acting as a dumping ground for the excluded pupils no other school

wanted, it is small wonder that it is marred by poor truancy figures and exam results.

But this need not be the end for Village School and its proud 63-year history.

The formal public notice of the proposed closure has still not been published. The council may have started drawing up plans for new classrooms and catchment areas elsewhere but all objections must be considered through an independent committee.

Which means that there is still time to back the Save Our School campaign, urging the city council to rethink its strategy and look for ways to keep a pared-down Village Community School.

Together we can force the politicians to listen to the people.

ARE PLAYING FIELDS THE REAL REASON BEHIND PROPOSALS TO AXE VILLAGE SCHOOL? PAGES 6&7

INSIDE: National News 2 ■ Letters 4 ■ Brennan 14 ■ TV/Radio 24 ■ Puzzles and Information 26 ■ Classified 28 ■ Sport 42

BETRAYED

The people who control Derby's schools need to take some lessons in democracy.

That is the view of the hundreds of parents and residents who object to the decision by Derby City Council to close one of the city's oldest secondary schools.

Village Community School in Normanton seems destined to be killed off as the council attempts to deal with more than 2,000 surplus pupil places in Derby.

The authority has decided that, from September of next year, Village's 500 pupils will be divided between two other schools with surplus places – Bemrose and Sinfin Community Schools.

Those who have protested at the closure decision feel betrayed by the system of public 'consultation' that led to the school's demise and by the fact that their views were swept aside by the people who carried out the consultation.

They feel betrayed because they cannot turn to the councillors they elected – council leader Robert Jones and his deputy Chris Williamson – because they are among the decision-makers who have signed Village Community School's death warrant.

In short, although they have formed a Save Our School action group, the protestors feel powerless in their desire to urge the council to rethink its strategy and look for ways to keep open this vital education link in what is already a socially deprived community.

Which is why, today, the Derby Evening Telegraph is speaking up for the 1,500 people who have protested at the closure and feel that the council has not listened to their views.

On their behalf, we ask the council some basic questions about its decision.

No one is underestimating the problems at Village Community School, but after years of decline and acting as a dumping ground for the excluded pupils no other school wanted, it is small wonder that it is marred by poor truancy figures and exam results.

But this need not be the end for Village School and its proud 63-year history.

The formal public notice of the proposed closure has still not been published. The council may have started drawing up plans for new classrooms and catchment areas elsewhere but all objections must be considered through an independent committee.

Which means that there is still time to back the Save Our School campaign, urging the city council to rethink its strategy and look for ways to keep a pared-down Village Community School.

Together we can force the politicians to listen to the people.

Answers to the Village School questions that matter

Parents of pupils at Village Community School are campaigning to try to overcome a proposal by Derby City Council to close their school next year.

Last week the Derby Evening Telegraph, shocked by the lack of information from the council and apparent disregard of parents' opinions, launched its own campaign of support. Eight days ago we put a series of questions about the situation to the city council which has now issued a response from Councillor Hardyal Dhindsa, lead member for lifelong learning.

The questions we asked on behalf of the parents

These are the questions we asked the city council on behalf of parents.

We had hoped that the questions would be answered individually but this was not the case.

By re-printing them, readers can follow why specific points have been picked up in the answer.

- The Closure of Village School was just one option among five. Why did the council opt for it when the majority of responses to the consultation – including those of leading teaching unions – favoured keeping the school open and scaling it down?
- Why did the council belittle the petition so much?
- How much will it cost to close Village Community School and how will the council pay for it?
- What will happen to the school site and its playing fields?
- What will happen to pupils in important exam years?
- How much will it cost to refurbish Bemrose and Sinfin?
- How will the other pupils be split fairly between Bemrose and Sinfin.
- Will the council pay the transport costs of pupils who are forced to go to other schools?
- How much would it cost to keep Village Community School open and lose the surplus places at the other schools in the city?
- How long have you been planning to close the school and how influential was Simon Longley's damning report of the place last year?

Response from Councillor Hardyal Dhindsa, lead member for lifelong learning

"I have great sympathy with the parents who are concerned about the proposed closure of Village Community School.

I would have been surprised if they had not felt this way, and in their situation I would probably have taken the same action.

The council wanted to consider views from all interested parties and always said this would be the case. The parents' petition was not belittled.

All of us involved in the process could not fail to recognise the strength of support expressed through the petition and it was clearly reported to the policy (education) committee.

However, reference also needed to be made to some questionable aspects, whilst pointing out that this hardly diminished its strength.

I am particularly interested and concerned that pupils in our schools, including those in Village School, receive the best education we can provide. I attended Village School when it was called Homelands and would have been the first to try and find an option following the city council to keep the school open.

However, the problem we face is that, if that were to be done, even as a small school, it would not lead to achieving the three objectives we set for the reorganisation during the consultation.

These were that any proposals should:

- Remove surplus places;
- Use available funds more effectively across our schools and most important of all;
- Result in a positive impact on education.

The option chosen is the one that can deliver these, based on best professional service.

I was well aware that whichever option the council chose would have been unpopular with some sections of the public.

However, as politicians, there are times when unpopular decisions have to be made, to achieve, the best overall outcomes. In the end, democracy is about making long-term policy decisions in the interests of service users and the city as a whole.

I want to explain the background to the decision and answer the questions raised in the Derby Evening Telegraph.

Some of these were covered in the report to the policy (education) committee in September, when it was also noted that many of the issues relating to implementation would be covered in the November meeting.

First, the issue is not simply a question of money. All councils work within limited budgets and it is our job to make sure we use the available funding as effectively as possible. This is clearly not the case where there are small schools and surplus places, resulting in a wide disparity of funding in the city's schools.

The council did ask Department for Education and Employment officials about the possibility of funding option 2. A firm answer is never given in these situations and at this stage.

However, the criteria by which the Government will provide resources to upgrade buildings and support school developments are quite clear. They do not include maintaining three small schools with large numbers of surplus places and difficulties in providing a full range of opportunities and high standards of achievement for their students. In fact, efforts were made in the last year to obtain extra funds for Village School, but without success.

The cost of closing Village School will depend on decisions about support to pupils and staff and transport. The costs were estimated in the report to policy (education) committee at £44,000 in the first year plus any costs of staff retirement/redundancy, or relating to buildings, but these would then decrease over years.

Much also depends on the future of the buildings and site. Against this, there will be an estimated £210,000 per year in savings, which can ultimately be used more effectively across more schools, and this figure rises to £359,000 in a full year. This could narrow the gap between the highest and lowest funded schools by around £200 per pupil (around 20 per cent).

The estimated costs of refurbishing Bemrose and Sinfin are £1.2 million and £1 million respectively, but these costs can be met by:

- Borrowing approvals, if the Government regards the proposals as effective in removing surplus places and improving;
- Any receipt from selling the school site or part of it: this would mean we would not have to borrow as much money, but as outlined below, we would prefer to use the site for other purposes.

Keeping Village open and losing surplus places at other schools would mean demolishing or taking out of use facilities at the three schools concerned. The building work at Village alone is estimated at between £1m and £1.5m, for which there would be no borrowing approval from Government, and this option would not necessarily improve educational opportunities.

It would also mean the difference in funding each pupil across Derby schools would remain high and, unlike Village the other schools do not have separate buildings that could easily be taken out of use.

Schools also have to be funded by a formula, with a limited ability to add extra to individual schools in what the Evening telegraph calls 'an enlightened approach'. The council is quite that pupils in areas such as those served by Village, Bemrose and Sinfin do need extra resources.

Village School has had extra funding as a small school and in recognition of the needs of that part of the city. However, after a number of years of great effort by the school, parents and the city council, they have not realised the educational improvement to persuade more parents to choose the school. In fact, the opposite has occurred and there have to be limits to what more can be done.

The comparison with the size of the school in 1938 is misleading as the two schools are completely different. Village was previously a girls' grammar school.

It is suggested that the situation will simply occur again in the future at Bemrose and Sinfin. Our proposals will fill current surplus places at the two schools and provide better curriculum coverage and opportunities, because of the resources available to larger schools. It will also make more resources available to all our schools. If we keep open three schools with too many places and spread insufficient pupils amongst them, the situation can only become worse.

It has been said that opening up the site for other educational purpose would be 'rubbing the local community's noses in it'. I do not feel that this is the case.

I believe there is a great need for a facility in the area which responds to identified need. This could include early years provision, youth services and family support, lifelong learning opportunities for adults, or possibly a homework centre, as well as access to public open space.

These are crucial service needs, which I passionately believe should be met here, and I will do all I can to make sure this happens.

This has to be in partnership with other providers, such as the colleges as the council cannot do it alone.

If it is not possible, then the last and worst option is to sell the site or part of it.

If so, there would be further consultation, on the use of the site in future.

The need to support students in the transition period, particularly those in the exam years, is recognised.

We are talking about the best way of doing this, linked to how we will support staff in finding new jobs.

I personally have met with the headteachers and chairs of governors of the three schools identified in the consultation process to progress these issues.

The law relating to admissions means students cannot simply be divided between Bemrose and Sinfin, just as it has been impossible to keep up pupil members at Village. Parents have the right to express a preference. However, as far as possible within the system, we will make sure we allocate pupils from the areas concerned as evenly as possible between the remaining schools.

We will consider transport costs, but there are many students who already have to walk or travel up to three miles to their secondary schools. Free transport is not provided for them. However, as reported to policy (education) committee, in recognition of the disruption caused by the council's decision, a hardship fund is being considered to respond to individual need for transport and uniform changes without compromising current council policy.

The council had no plans to close Village School until we made the decision at the end of the consultation.

The report on Village School, referred to in the article, was part of the support and intervention processes that are expected by the Government from a local education authority.

It did not directly influence the decision, though educational performance was clearly a factor we took into account.

All of us at the city council recognise that closing a school is an unhappy situation for any community, but we are convinced that it is the best way of improving opportunities for our young people.

If there were another, better way to achieve this, we would have taken it. No option provides perfect or certain results but, in the light of all the factors, it was felt that this was the best one available. We now need to work to ensure its success.

Finally, on behalf of the city council, I can say we are happy to discuss and clarify any concerns raised by parents of pupils at Village School and would welcome contact."

Our response to the reply

COUNCILLOR Hardyal Dhindsa appears to have totally underestimated the "unhappy situation" that exists in the community around Normanton.

When he eventually gets around to meeting the parents and children whose lives will be affected if the proposed closure of Village Community School goes ahead, he will be left in no doubt as to how unhappy they feel.

Mr Dhindsa's response to our questions is well-written but some elements of the community may find it difficult to follow the arguments he puts forward.

Indeed, we find it difficult to find anything new in the response that hasn't been trotted out at consultation meetings. They are mainly words without specific answers but with solemn political overtones.

In fact, the response seems to raise more questions than it answers and issues such as transport, the future for exam stage students and how pupils will be fairly split between the Bemrose and Sinfin schools are still unresolved.

Quite rightly, the parents feel that they are still no wiser about the future. But the bottom line is that they don't want their school to close.

And with it costing £2.2m to refurbish Bemrose and Sinfin Community schools, they cannot understand why the cheaper option of keeping Village Community is being ignored.

Talk of a better education in a larger school is lost on the parents because they already feel they are working with some of the finest teachers.

It's very hard for parents to understand that money is not at the bottom of this decision, when the financial situation is mentioned several times as justification for closure.

For those in the community, and further afield, there is no reassurance that the school and its playing fields will not eventually be sold off.

But the local community, already concerned about the school consultation process, needn't worry because 'there would be further consultation on the use of the site in the future'.

It would have been more reassuring to have read that the council was prepared to reconsider its decision to close the school.

According to the council, the Government has never ruled out the possibility of keeping the school open because it never gave an answer to the question of funding the option.

Mr Dhindsa must know that they are not about to drop their campaign, but are determined to see the school stay open.

Derby Evening Telegraph – Friday 13th October 2000

72

My Friends and Other Pupils

The group of scholarship girls who travelled from Melbourne to Homelands in September 1942 was amongst the first from the village to attend that school; previously grammar school girls had attended Parkfields Cedars. Two of the girls who went at that time were already friends of mine: Olive Cooper and Doreen Tivey. Sylvia Haslam was also a friend in the early years and went on some expeditions in the car with my parents and myself. Olive and Doreen still live locally, but Sylvia (I am told) went to Birmingham, married a bank manager and had three children. I remember her for her extraordinarily beautiful dark plaits. Then there were the Earp sisters, Diana and Veronica, both now dead. My memory of these contemporaries has faded over the years, because we did not progress through the school together. When I was in the second form something happened which resulted in a complete change of friends. I had rheumatic fever and, because from March 1944 onwards in that academic year I was off school, when I returned in September I rejoined in the second form, with a different group of girls. (I suspect one of the causes of the rheumatic fever was the nights we spent in the damp cellar at home when the air raid alerts were on.) A minor (although not minor to me) result of this repeated year was that I did not have the chance to learn Latin. The first time round, we were given the choice of Latin, Domestic Science or something called (I think) Special Preparation, whatever that was. I chose Latin, but when I returned the following September that option was no longer open. To this day I feel deprived, although my friends assure me I haven't missed a thing. Most of the friendships formed from 1944 onwards have survived, but my friends will be horrified to know that I cannot put a date on when the group known as The Gang came into being. (Doubtless one or more of them will be able to provide an accurate date.) One 'best friend' did continue in that capacity from when we were friends together in the first form: Joan Ashley. I remember writing lengthy letters to her while I was in hospital and she certainly continued as a member of The Gang until after School Certificate. She and I are now on Christmas card terms (my fault), but the rest of us are still together after more than fifty years (and many vicissitudes).

The Gang was certainly in existence by the fourth form, because that was when the alleged 'scowling' behaviour of Joyce Mercer and me during Miss Robinson's French lessons occurred. The Gang comprises June Allen (known as Jally), Margaret Flatt (known as Flatty), Stella Clarricoats (known sometimes as Beetle and sometimes as Clarry), Dorothy Perkins (known as Kitten), Joyce Mercer (known as Beltane), Pat Broadbent and me (known as Tantor, because of my elephantine size). Some members of The Gang left after School Certificate, but my recollection is that we still met until those who went into the sixth form took Higher School Certificate. Thereafter, although I remember corresponding with Margaret, in particular, while we were both at college, various schisms took place. The other members may or may not touch on these matters. In my case the rot set in with marriage. I quarrelled with Pat before my marriage and lost touch with everyone else after it. (I was married, at far too young an age, in 1953. Of course, by then, having left home in 1950, I thought I knew all the answers.) This gap in my friendship with members of The Gang lasted until 1979, when I returned to work in Derby and to live in Melbourne. St. Helen's House, where I worked for the Workers' Educational Association, also housed the Teachers' Centre, and one day June sought me out in the building.

We also met accidentally at Horncastle College, where we were attending residential courses organised by our respective employers. I am not entirely sure whether it was the meeting in St. Helen's House, the meeting at Horncastle College, or an article in the Derby Evening Telegraph which included a photograph of me ('Can that be <u>our</u> Marjorie?' one or two members of The Gang wondered) that triggered my return to the fold. Whichever it was, I shall be eternally grateful to my friends for welcoming me back. While we were all working, the annual Christmas reunions were a great joy. Now we are retired our meetings are more frequent; some of The Gang (the numbers vary) make enjoyable excursions here, there and everywhere throughout the year.

Apart from the members of The Gang, few other pupils at the school left any lasting impression on me. At one stage I was friendly with a girl called Margaret Girvan, but the friendship didn't last very long (I've no idea why). I remember a Head Girl called – improbably – Meta Bull. Inevitably, because we both did Chemistry in the sixth form, Vera Seago and I were thrown together quite a lot, but we were never kindred spirits. Years later, in the 1980s and 1990s, Vera used to return to Derby specially for the wonderful coffee mornings that Grace Graham and Kathleen Robinson used to hold once a year at their home in Warwick Avenue, in aid of charity. Vera had kept in touch with Noreen Woods, another sixth form contemporary whose main subjects were Pure and Applied Mathematics and who went on to become a Deputy Head Teacher. Pure Mathematics, even when taught by Grace Graham, was more than enough for me; my third subject for Higher School Certificate was Physics.

Form 4A, July 1947
(Form Mistress Grace Graham back row extreme right)

Photograph courtesy of Marjorie Calow

Social Activities

Rather surprisingly, since music was, and is, one of my passions, I didn't join the school choir, although I loved to join in the hymns during daily Assembly and to sing with everyone else at Speech Day. The annual carol service at St. Giles's Church was also an annual treat. Perhaps my lack of participation in the choir was due to the length of the journey between Melbourne and Derby. I didn't take part in any of the school plays (always performed in November, with the inevitable risk of fog) either, although I now know that Grace Graham and Kathleen Robinson went to endless pains with the productions, not least because they researched the costumes meticulously, even consulting the archives at Chatsworth House on one occasion. Needless to say, I avoided any sporting activities, such as Saturday matches, like the plague.

The school was divided into five houses, named after famous Derbyshire families. I was in Babington; Spencer was one of the others, but I can't remember the names of the other three. All the houses had shields; when the school ceased to exist as Homelands, Grace and Kathleen acquired the shields, but their current whereabouts are unknown to me. On balance I was not in favour of the house system, since one couldn't choose which house to be in and none of my friends were in Babington. This became important at Christmas, because each house had a separate party; members of staff were also allocated to houses. My recollection of the parties is that I was bored. But, once again, memory fails: I cannot remember what we did at the parties, or whether food was involved. At some stage boys were invited from Bemrose (the boys' grammar school) to help us learn ballroom dancing, but this might have been a separate sixth form activity. Whenever it was, being fat and ugly, I hated it; I didn't want to learn ballroom dancing anyway. We certainly had lessons when no boys were present and one girl had to take the male lead. When I saw the film of *The Prime of Miss Jean Brodie* the ballroom dancing scene provoked a wry smile of recognition.

I remember a great sense of excitement about Speech Days. We all did our best to look smart. My memory of Speech Days when I was in the sixth form is of wearing a black skirt, white blouse and school tie. The uniform up to the sixth form was a black gym tunic and white blouse. In summer we wore light blue dresses with beige trimmings. Out of doors we wore dark coats or blazers, with a velour hat in winter and a straw hat in summer. Although I didn't mind the uniform in general, I hated the hats (particularly the straw ones). However, if we were caught (or were reported) in the street without a hat we were disciplined. At Speech Day the hall was full of serried ranks of well-scrubbed, smiling school girls and the balcony was full of proud parents (who were allowed to chat to the staff after the formal proceedings). The staff wore their academic gowns and hoods and there was much speculation concerning the provenance of the differently coloured hoods. The platform party comprised various local dignitaries (including the mayor, complete with chain of office), the headmistress and the guest speaker, who presented the prizes. In addition to his speech (it was usually, if not always, a man) we had speeches from the other worthies. Sometimes they were (at least to a critical and obnoxious adolescent like myself) cringe-making, as when one good lady said "'ow 'appy we are to 'ave Sir 'Ector 'Etherington with us today".

Little did I realise that it was probably the vision of such ladies as that one who had caused Homelands to come into being. Girls who had won prizes collected them from the platform and shook hands with the speaker in the time-honoured fashion. Since it all went very smoothly I think we must have rehearsed in the morning, but, to my shame, I cannot remember the precise nature of the informal proceedings afterwards.

As I have already mentioned, we were taken to an art exhibition on one occasion. We also went to see at least two films during school hours. Scott of the Antarctic bored me; I hate snow and have no interest in exploration. This was, of course, a philistine reaction; at that age I didn't even appreciate the grandeur of Vaughan Williams's music. Equally philistine was my reaction to Henry V (the Olivier version). All I remember is the question asked by the Duke Of Orleans: 'Will it never be morning?' (Act III, Scene VII). My (silent) question was: 'Will this film never end?' From the perspective of the twenty-first century, I now know that we were being subjected to a bit of war-time propaganda. (This is not a judgemental comment. I simply find it fascinating to note that this was the case, having seen recent productions of *Henry V* in which the English in general and the King in particular are presented in a less flattering light.) Be that as it may, the film was my first introduction to Shakespeare performance and I don't think it did me any harm in the long run.

By far the most important social activity of my school days did not, however, take place until I was in the sixth form. During those years, Grace Graham and Kathleen Robinson held play readings at the large house in Duffield Road where Grace lodged with Miss Haslam. (This was before Grace and Kathleen set up home together in Warwick Avenue.) We certainly read *The Happiest Days of Your Life* and a play by Christopher Fry (*The Lady's not for Burning*, perhaps). We all read a part, including Grace and Kathleen. Afterwards there was wonderful food; Grace and Kathleen always excelled at hospitality. How <u>very</u> kind they were. The experience certainly opened a window onto a different world for me. I think I appreciated these events at the time. The last one for me was during the summer before I left school to attend university. In those days there were plenty of buses and girls of my age could travel safely in the late evening. I have a clear recollection that, as I sat on the bus taking me into the centre of Derby, where I would catch the last bus home, I shed real tears, because I knew that an era had come to an end for me.

Stratford, June 1950
Margaret, Stella, Marjorie
Photograph courtesy of Marjorie Calow

76

Rhona (née Wilson) Haywood

Happy memories of Homelands School 70 years after it was founded
just a year before the war

I ALWAYS liked school. From the National School at Alvaston, I could not have made a better choice than Homelands Grammar School.

It was built in 1938, with a Georgian look, the epitome of functional elegance. The parquet-floored hall, with a stage at one end and a balcony at the other, was used for prayers, performances, speech days and ballroom dancing at dinner time 'if wet'.

Long, straight corridors looked out onto lawned quadrangles at one side and into classrooms at the other.

The gym, complete with showers and sick bay, had a beautifully sprung floor and the usual complement of wall bars, beams, ropes, horses and all the necessary items for the game of shipwrecks that we played at the end of one term.

That name was unfortunate during those war years, with many ships and lives lost at sea. I don't remember playing it again.

The day before the school year started, we first-formers, in 1942, assembled in the hall and were introduced to our form mistresses. There were 30 girls in each form – 1a, 1b, and 1c – according to age. Then we were assigned to our houses; mine was Darwin.

It soon became clear that 'recess' must be said instead of 'playtime' and 'May I be excused' rather than 'May I leave the room'.

And on no account should you ever address a teacher as 'Miss', without adding her surname. Running in the corridors was forbidden and indoor shoes had always to be worn in the building.

In form 1a, subjects included ancient Egyptian history, the book, *The Wind in the Willows*, and how to dance the veleta, quickstep and square tango. Mrs Arter, our form-mistress, was a well-known Derby ballroom dancer.

At that time, Miss Welbank was headmistress. When you were given a point for a good piece of work, you had to queue outside her office for her signature and the point would go to the credit of your house.

Form 2s had Miss Steele's science lab as its form room. We learned how to turn white copper sulphate blue and about the 'anomalous expansion of water on freezing'.

We took Domestic Science and needlework during that year and then had to decide whether or not to include it as a career choice. We each concocted a meat stew and lemon meringue pie, and sewed a cookery apron, knickers and a smocked blouse. I opted for Maths and Science.

I enjoyed playing the position of centre in the school junior netball team and playing in matches against other Derbyshire schools.

The choice of games was between netball and hockey. Our playing fields were spacious, even allowing for the air raid shelters dug out of them, although we had no tennis courts and had to walk to Normanton Rec sometimes for lessons.

We never had to use the air raid shelters, thank goodness, as I doubt if we would have made it in time. I think it was still the period when we had to carry our gas masks around.

Homelands House had been the dwelling of the original owners. It was reached from the main building by a covered way, which was supported by brick pillars festooned with climbing roses. It had a garden at the back, with a lawn and tennis court, which was used by some of the mistresses now and then.

Homelands House, Old Normanton

Photograph courtesy of Normanton-by-Derby Local History Group

School dinners were eaten in the house, at tables for ten, with a fifth or sixth-former at the head, graduating to a first-former at the foot. Two servers from each table brought over the serving dishes.

The school stew, with chunks of swede, and semolina pudding were both hated but treacle tart made with oats, chipped out of the tin like bits of shrapnel, was cordially welcomed and the occasional wasp in the stewed plums was really exciting.

The dining room was quite spacious and music lessons were held at one end, where Miss Newman reigned with her piano.

I have their influence to thank for my visits to Derby Grand Theatre to see a young Margot Fonteyn and a very mature Robert Helpmann dance roles in *Les Sylphides*, *Coppelia*, *Spectre de la Rose*, *The Rake's Progress*, *The Nutcracker*, etc, with the wonderful Sadlers' Wells Ballet company. My classmates and I used to queue for the 'gods', the cheapest seats with the best views.

Upstairs in the old house were the ovens and scrubbed tables for Domestic Science lessons. By the third form, we had a new headmistress, Miss Gilbert, who came to us from Cheltenham Ladies College.

She upgraded our navy-blue blazers to royal blue with a white 'Buck in the Park' on the pocket, with matching royal blue berets and scarves with white stripes. Possibly we were not quite her scene, for she did not stay with us for long.

At the end of that year, we had to choose between Geography and History as a school certificate subject. I did Geography.

Miss Dawson offered to take some of our Form 4a on a Geography walk in the Manifold and Dove dales, overnighting at the youth hostel at Ilam Hall.

About 10 of us accepted, eager to see and learn about the effects of sun, rain and wind action on limestone – the crags, meanders, the swallow holes, where streams disappear underground, etc. It was a wonderful trip with the rain holding off until we waited for the bus homeward.

For the history of architecture, we visited and sketched Derby Cathedral tower, Repton Church's Saxon crypt and Southwell Minster, which I consider had the most beautiful interior I had ever seen.

Our art mistress, Miss Marion Adnams, was a noted painter and also produced intricate figures made of card. I saw one of her paintings exhibited at Derby Art Gallery recently and must confess I was still a bit puzzled about it.

The 1964 extension to the original building
Derby Museum and Art Gallery
Image Source: Wikipedia

In Form 5a, I took my General School Certificate exams. There must have been a spell of hot, dry weather in June because I remember that my two good friends, Joan and Edna, and I sat around in a nearby pasture one day, more or less revising.

I cannot recall anyone in our group getting especially anxious about sitting the exams or waiting for results, although it could have been that we were less demonstrative then.

We needed a minimum of five passes to get a General School Certificate and to add Matriculation Exemption (the stepping stone to university), you had to achieve five credits, including English and maths or science.

We were invited to leave at school a stamped, addressed postcard, with our subject titles listed, which would be posted to us with our passes and grades written on it.

The ambience in the Lower Sixth was probably less formal but I think we all worked hard at our subjects. My particular interests were English, French literature, and Geography.

The Upper Sixth put on a performance of Moliere's *Le Malade Imaginaire* and I almost felt honoured when they asked me to speak the prologue.

Miss Helmore, a tall, white-haired figure, was our much-respected headmistress at that time.

We seemed to have quite a high turnover of teachers over six or seven years, perhaps due to reasons connected with the war.

Dr Rae, who taught German and Latin, had spent several years in Germany during the early 1930s and had her hair plaited into 'earphones'. She was quite elegant and was the only mistress to wear her gown habitually, though not a mortarboard.

Mr Ribbons, our only male teacher, came out of the RAF and always wore his 'sheepskin liberty bodice', a sleeveless sheepskin jacket. I think he may have worn his gown now and then.

Miss Cousins arrived straight from Oxford.

Mrs Blaine taught mathematics and eventually rejoined her husband at their farm.

Miss Land taught physical education for years and could seem quite draconian to juniors but was well liked and respected, as we got older. When one of our junior netball team explained that she could not be there for the Saturday morning practice, Miss Land was adamant that it was impossible for her to keep her place in the team, despite her reason for absence. The girl's mother, who went out to work, insisted she needed help in the house on Saturdays.

When Miss Land died a few years after we had left, we contributed towards a rose garden for her in the front drive.

I had a great admiration for two of the girls I knew well, who got their BSc through evening classes at Derby Technical College, and being given day release by their employers. They were Margaret, who qualified as a pharmacist, and Rosemary, who landed a good job with the railway company she worked for. I also admired Mary McLean, who won a place at Oxford, and apparently, was good at everything.

I always liked school – especially Homelands.

Derby Evening Telegraph – Monday 15th September 2008

DOROTHY'S DISCOURSE

Dorothy M (née Perkins) Padmore

The Homelands uniform dress of royal blue cotton, button-through with white collar and cuffs, was the most desirable fashion garment to junior school girls, especially in the wartime climate of 'Make Do and Mend', but to have the privilege of wearing it first had to pass an examination, universally known as 'the scholarship'. (At that time Homelands was still a fee-paying school; not until the Butler Act of 1944 were fees abolished.)

After weeks of anxious waiting, our junior school teacher announced the exam results and I heard with great relief and excitement that I was one of the twenty-one girls from the school offered a place at Homelands. The teacher went on to say that a twenty-second name was on the list but had to be confirmed. Shortly afterwards the last name was announced. It was a surprise when the name was verified, as the girl did not shine academically. On the morning of our first day we arrived at the main gates of the school in Village Street and were directed up the west drive, but this girl walked slowly up the main drive flanked by her parents, their faces filled with delight, pride and awe. This remains my only clear memory of my first day at Homelands. Some thirty years later I met this girl again, a smartly dressed, well-spoken woman who had just been awarded a degree.

I had expected to start school wearing a royal blue dress but the dress code for the Autumn and Spring terms dictated a navy tunic, white shirt blouse and royal blue pullover. These were worn with either grey woollen knee socks or fawn lisle stockings, the latter a great improvement on the dark brown or black woollen stockings of junior school. Winter outdoor wear was a navy coat or gaberdine raincoat with a navy velour hat, the hat band striped in the school colours of navy and royal blue with the multicoloured 'Buck in the Park' shield badge in the centre. A knitted woollen hat with the shield at the front was the permitted alternative chosen by most girls. Hat and gloves were mandatory; any girl seen outside the school gates in school uniform without a hat received a punishment of order marks or lines.

On entering school each morning and afternoon we changed from black outdoor shoes to black button-strap house shoes, essential to protect the well-maintained polished wood floors of corridors and classrooms. This discipline was well absorbed, for even now I change my shoes when I arrive home (and also never feel properly dressed without gloves, though I always did rebel against wearing a hat).

We had to wait until the summer term to wear the coveted blue dress. There were three designs: an early-thirties drop-waisted pattern, which was never seen; a waisted version, which was worn by some of the older (former Central School) girls; and the button-through design chosen by most new entrants. The dress (and winter tunic) had to brush the floor when the wearer was kneeling, though wartime clothes rationing caused the relaxation of this requirement to permit a length of up to five inches from the floor when kneeling.

The dress was worn with a navy blazer sporting the badge on the pocket and a panama hat with the school hatband. White ankle socks replaced the fawn stockings.

The first headmistress was the formidable Miss Welbank, a small, thin lady with white hair drawn back in a bun who seemed ancient to first formers. With a forbidding manner she held total sway over the school with the invaluable support of the very efficient, approachable and ever-cheerful school secretary, Miss Orton. When we were in the second form Miss Welbank retired, to be replaced by the mercurial Miss Gilbert, a sharp-mannered, stocky woman who wore her straight dark hair shingled. She proceeded to dismantle the last remnants of the old Central School from which Homelands was created. Typewriting had already been phased out; Domestic Science and Needlework were banished to allow far greater emphasis on academic subjects; Latin was added to the curriculum and only then did we truly appreciate that learning another language helped to improve knowledge and understanding of the English language, grammar and usage. Miss Gilbert also introduced Kipling's stirring 'Non Nobis Domine' as the school song and changed the school colours to royal blue and white. The button-through dress became the standard summer uniform with a royal blue blazer; the 'buck in the park' became white on royal blue; panama, velour and knitted woollen hats were quietly dropped in favour of a royal blue beret with blue and white shield badge. Miss Gilbert reigned for just over a year, leaving on her appointment as a school inspector. Her successor, Miss Helmore, was the calm after the storm.

Newspaper cutting courtesy of Marjorie Calow

On our first day the school seemed vast and the layout confusing. We gazed in admiration at the Saturn-ringed light suspended in the stairwell at the front entrance; the quiet library; the exciting science labs; the east and west quadrangles (always off bounds unless checking the weather station) and between them the daunting gym with changing rooms and shower block attached.

The gym could only be entered in Plimsolls. As these were unobtainable in wartime we had our gym lessons barefooted, resulting in an epidemic of verrucae. We had a second chance to collect a verruca in swimming lessons at the old Reginald Street baths. We walked from school to the baths and, as rubber swimming caps were unobtainable, walked home with wet hair, whatever the outdoor temperature.

The annual Swimming Gala at Reginald Street was a noisy affair contested by the Houses to which we were allocated in our first week. These were named after famous Derbyshire personalities: Arkwright, house colour red; Babington, purple; Darwin, orange; Nightingale, green; Spencer, blue. The Houses also competed on Sports Day and at the end of term when order marks, handed out for bad behaviour and rule-breaking, were totted up.

On the sports field the school teams played matches against other local schools: deep gloom descended on the school at Morning Assembly if there was an announcement by the Head Girl that a Homelands team had lost to deadly rivals Parkfields Cedars. At Morning Assembly, for several years, the piano was played by Vida Hand and Margaret Pitt, two brilliant pianists who could tackle any music set before them. The most memorable Head Girl was Pat Shepard who became known as Lady Macbeth following her commanding performance in the school play. The quality of school plays varied widely. All subsequent versions of Macbeth, amateur and professional, have brought back the memory of the ghosts wafting across the back of the Homelands stage: the ghosts changed, unlike their car-rug tartans which each gave several encores.

Speech Days tend to be remembered for all the wrong reasons. Who could forget the Mayor introducing the principal speaker, Sir 'Ector 'Etherington; or another Mayor who had 'never 'eard girls sing so beautiful in all my life'.

Speech Day 1948 Miss M. P. Helmore with Sir Hector Hetherington
Photograph courtesy of Derby Evening Telegraph

The school was politically correct long before that phrase had been coined: our chalk was royal blue, used on primrose boards. The chalk dust covered everything with a blue film, not least the teachers' clothes. Another of Headmistress Gilbert's reforms was the replacement of primrose and blue with conventional black and white.

While the war in no way affected the quality of our schooling, it did affect the routine. Each form was allocated to an air-raid shelter. These dark, dank, underground bunkers were situated at the rear of the school, at right angles to the building. In addition to tire drill, air-raid drill was a feature of school life in our first two years, though I only recall one occasion when we needed to take to the shelters 'for real'. We created gardens on the earth mounds over the shelters, bringing plants from home and weeding the plots at lunchtime and also at recess in summer if we had any time to spare after we had walked along the covered way to Homelands House for the daily bottle of milk. The crates were left outside in the sun and inevitably on warm days the milk was unpleasantly sour by mid-morning recess.

In the first week or two of the Autumn Term any spare time was devoted to scouring the lawns under the large horse chestnut trees for conkers. At this time of year the most popular girls were those from the Melbourne area who brought in large bags of sweet chestnuts gathered from trees around the Melbourne to Breedon footpath.

Homelands House was the former residence of Giles Austin, the owner of Austin's (later Austin Hodgkinson's) High Class Grocery Store, originally sited on Full Street, later moving to the west side of the Market Place. On his death the Derby Borough Council acquired the property. The School was constructed on a 25-acre section of the estate adjoining Homelands House. In June 1937, Alderman Mrs Elizabeth Petty laid the foundation stone for the school which was built at a cost of £90,000. The school opened in September 1938.

Mr Giles Austin Tea Tasting, Normanton-by-Derby, *c*1920

Photograph courtesy of Normanton-by-Derby Local History Group

Domestic Science lessons were taught in Homelands House under the benign eye of Miss Coulson who lived in a flat in the house. Groups of pupils were taken to the flat to learn such household tasks as bed-making, laundry and ironing. Many ingredients for cookery were rationed but the school had a limited supply of some items for educational use: these Miss Coulson measured out with great precision. She delighted in methods for the various tasks, in particular the regularly repeated order for washing up: glass; cutlery; tableware; pots and pans. On occasion, in summer, a lesson would be abandoned for us to gather fruit such as blackcurrants from the kitchen garden of Homelands House. These fruits were conserved for use in the refectory.

Normanton House, on the eastern side of the school, housed Italian prisoners of war. The land along the boundary was strictly out of bounds.

Normanton House, Normanton by Derby, *c*1910

Photograph courtesy of Normanton-by-Derby Local History Group

In the 1740s the Dixie family had Normanton Hall built; this was later used as a school building in the 20th century.

As the war neared its end we were taught the National Anthems of all our Allies. On the day of the announcement of the cessation of hostilities in Europe the entire school gathered in the hall to sing all these anthems.

Our teachers were superb, dedicated, and in the early years were nearly all spinsters. Miss Welbank was a remote but respected Head. Miss Yates, a tiny white-haired veteran from the old Central School, was an excellent teacher of French whose stern application of discipline and ready distribution of order marks earned her the sobriquet 'Lion of the Top Corridor'. On well-earned retirement she was replaced by Kathleen Robinson who shared French teaching with the long-serving Evelyn Loydall, both greatly respected.

In the fifth form we were appalled to learn that we were to be taught French by Miss Finniecome, a new young teacher. From the beginning she struggled to maintain order in a form, which had no history of rowdyism.

The situation deteriorated until the day we took the seat pad from her chair. She entered the room, pulled the chair away from her desk and without looking sat down and went straight through. The form had not anticipated this and, as she extricated herself, we stood in horrified silence awaiting the sentence, which would inevitably be passed on us. The poor lady pushed away the offending chair, pulled another from an empty desk, then started the lesson as if nothing untoward had occurred. Maybe our obvious horror persuaded her we were guiltless for the incident was never referred to. For the rest of the year Miss Finniecome taught a quiet, attentive, studious class and her ability was rewarded by most of the form achieving Distinction in School Certificate French.

Miss Moore, a serious lady with grey clothes and grey persona, taught Scripture and not until we met at Old Girls' events did I realise that she had a brilliant line in repartee. Miss Celia Hughes's first form English Literature lessons were a delight and from her part-reading of *Wind in the Willows* she has remained my definitive Mole.

Miss Jewsbury was the well-loved History teacher whose assumption that all her pupils would work conscientiously and achieve good results brought out the best in them and in return gave them total confidence in her. We were devastated when she left to become Head of History and Deputy Head at Oakham College. We had scant respect for her (mercifully temporary) replacement, Miss Wilson, known as 'Juicy' (D'you see) who rapidly gained a reputation for eccentric traits – one such being the scurrilous allegation from her pupils that she laid a paper trail to find her way around the building.

Miss Steel took Science. She was a tall, spare, softly-spoken Scotswoman whose teaching methods made Science easy. Her Astronomy lessons aroused in my friend June and myself a deep interest in the subject that lasts to this day, though my friend's long-suffering father and brother who were detailed by June's mother to accompany us on our youthful star-gazing expeditions in the blackout may not have held her in such high esteem.

Miss Land was the only car owner amongst the staff of that era. The long-serving Head of PE and demon checker of correct school uniform and name tags, she was a feared and daunting character but possessor of a soft side shown only to fifth and sixth formers. She also taught old-time and modern ballroom dancing. At the Christmas parties we had dance programmes, which we completed with the names of our pre-arranged dancing partners. In the higher forms, dancing skills were honed for the inter-school dances with boys from Bemrose School.

Miss Marion Adnams, Art, who died in 1995 at 96 years of age, was an artist of considerable merit whose surrealist works are still on show regularly in Derby Art Gallery. (One of her paintings, Alter Ego, was presented to the gallery by Headmistress Gilbert.)

Miss Adnams had little tolerance of girls with artistic talent whom she invariably adjudged to be under-using their gift but, as I discovered to my great advantage, she had infinite patience with the totally untalented. She made valiant efforts to pass on to them something of her skills and love of her subject. Her Architecture lessons opened up a new world, presenting a lifetime of interest to her pupils. One Easter the holiday task she set was the production of a detailed drawing of the Derby Cathedral tower. Several of us spent an intense morning sitting on the wall of the old Full Street Power Station making sketches for our masterpiece. Then we went inside the Cathedral and persuaded the Verger to let us climb to the top of the tower for a closer look at our subject.

Marion Adnams

Photograph courtesy of John V. Rooks

The artistic natures of Miss Adnams and Miss Rhoda Newman, Music, were possibly the reason that, to put it mildly, they were not the best of friends. Miss Newman usually brought laughter to her classes though on rare occasions some small irritation would trigger an explosion of rage. She also inflicted the greatest of torments on us: each girl had to sing a solo in class as an audition for the school choir no exception was permitted until I brought her to her knees.

Wincing at the sound I produced as singing, she stopped my solo after a few bars, grimly instructing me to continue in duet with another struggling soul. Needless to say the choir and I remained apart.

Towards the end of the school year in the fourth and fifth forms we had form outings. In July 1947, Miss Grace Graham, a superb Maths teacher and Form Mistress, together with Kathleen Robinson, took us to Haddon Hall. On the way home we started singing. This was suffered until we embarked on a raucous version of the then current popular song 'Open the door, Richard'. This brought a furious Miss Graham to her feet to remind us that we were Homelands Girls and should behave accordingly. Miss Robinson kept her head averted and I am convinced she was convulsed with laughter. In May 1948, Miss Olive Jones (who taught Geography) took us to Castleton to visit the Blue John caverns. The guide led us along the winding passage into the pitch-black cave with a powerful torch but the rest of us followed by the light of small candles; one shared by several girls. Halfway down we were ambushed by a party of small boys coming up. Their rearguard blew out our candles leaving us shrieking in the darkness.

St Giles's Church – Village Street

Image courtesy of K. S. Dhindsa © 2016

At the beginning and end of term we paraded to St. Giles's Church in Village Street. The services were conducted by the Reverend Turnbull who on one delightful occasion reduced us to barely concealed giggles by blessing the tadpoles. Our favourite service was the Christmas Carol Service when following lengthy coaching by Miss Newman we sang seasonal music in the decorated church. She also took some of us to the Cathedral to take part in the Derby Schools Carol Service.

There are so many memories of the school and the staff who inspired our studies, encouraged high standards of behaviour and opened our eyes and minds to an appreciation of the world about us. Above all, the greatest legacy for me without doubt has been the lasting friendship of fellow pupils, happily still strong nearly sixty years on. This is a treasure beyond price.

PAT'S PIECE
Pat Broadbent

My earliest memories of Homelands are of our form teacher with straight grey hair and severely cut tweed suit. She seemed very old; I had not met anyone like her before and I felt she had met no one like me either. I wondered why she smelled of coal dust (familiar to me, for coal fires were our main means of heating). I now realise that she probably lived in 'digs' and had to feed her own coal fire. Her single life may well have been bleak; by comparison business girls today have an easier time.

In my first year I was lonely. There were no 'playground friends' or 'friendship stations' about which I recently heard an enlightened headmaster talking. However this (to me) strange lady noticed my sadness. Another girl, who perhaps showed a similar tendency, and I were introduced to one another and we became firm friends. She was Margaret Fell. Unfortunately her family soon moved away I think to Coventry – and I gradually lost touch with her. Should she read this I would be pleased to have news of her. After this I apparently 'normalised' as I do not recall similar feelings again. From that first year I remember being completely baffled by blue chalk on yellow boards and having to sit at the back of the class because I was tall. From there I could not see the writing on the board but struggled on until a seat at the front and, later, spectacles cured the difficulty. It is easy to see why the elderly resist hearing aids long after they fail to hear adequately. We were brought up in that school of thought: we didn't complain.

During that year we had to draw an Egyptian mummy for this same teacher. It could not have been in Scripture so perhaps was part of a History lesson. I still wonder what purpose this served. It did fuel my interest in Ancient Egypt, only recently partly satisfied by a visit to Cairo and a cruise on the wonderful Nile.

History was still being taught as though it were about royalty and conquest with no thought of the people affected by war and political action. I remember wondering what happened to people in some of the sweeping statements told to us and felt sure that the Roundheads had a point of view even if everyone wanted to be a Royalist. Time alone has corrected the false view of history we were fed. People like Miss Witt are memorable for making us read 'Lepanto' and asking what we felt about it. Its rhythm and excitement have always stayed with me. I don't recall who directed us in a production of Macbeth, but I played one of the witches draped in a tartan blanket. Recently, seeing productions of the play in which the weird sisters evoke all types of modern depravity and in which Macbeth is no more than a thug, I wonder about the interpretation we studied, with Macbeth as some sort of politician or statesman.

One very snowy winter we had a party in the evening. I wore an itchy blue woollen dress with a belt I had embroidered myself (we had rationing and clothing coupons) and was one of the girls chosen to sit, for a time, and chat to Miss Helmore, the headmistress. Afterwards we walked home, probably three miles, a group of about six of us, singing all the way as we crunched through the hard, frozen ice and snow. Early impressions remained with me through life: I always enjoyed the English folk songs we learned and snow and walking have been a recurring pleasure.

The powers-who-were recognised our diverse backgrounds, so much so that we were taught in our first week how to politely manage cutlery at lunchtime. I remembered this years later when reading that Fidel Castro had all Cuban school children taught similarly so that they should not be disadvantaged. On balance I think the education offered served me well. It equipped me to earn a living, leaving me seeking knowledge and with wide interests. However I had turned sixty-five before I graduated. Yet perhaps even that would not have happened without the basics of a Homelands education.

I cannot be alone in recalling the awful experience of showers after gym and games. I hope such things are better managed these days. The misery of being a 'back' on the hockey field on a freezing winter day is very clear in my mind and what a long way it was from the bottom field to the warmth of the school building! Happier days were spent in the Old House where we learned cookery. The tennis courts adjoined this building and, perhaps in the summer holiday, we played there. I was never good enough to enjoy winning, but liked the place and its surrounding garden and the connecting 'covered way'. Within the warmth and home-like environment of the house we were taught not just cookery but laundry. I was incredulous that one should be taught how to wash clothes, a task which figured so large at home every week on Mondays. I loved our young Domestic Science teacher. My Eve's Pudding was a disaster – I still can't make a meringue but I got ten out of ten for my mince pies. As a vegetarian I shudder to recall that the pastry was made using lard!

After taking School Certificate I did not return as was planned. As the Summer Term drew to an end I remember feelings of impending disaster, which I have experienced prophetically on one or two occasions since. The upstairs classroom was deserted and seemed closer to the Scots Pines in the grounds than usual. The woodpigeons cooed noisily. Time seemed suspended. I did not return and have not been back to the school since. I regret its passing, feeling it deserved better. Its 1930s Corporation building style pleased me and I liked its composition-floored corridors and stone staircases.

From my time there I took a love of literature and geography. Compared with today's children we had lots of exercise, dancing, netball, hockey – and how we ran wild at lunchtimes in the early years I was at Homelands. In retrospect it seems like a fantasy with long paths to run over, large playing fields, space beneath big trees and at one boundary a copse of bushes and trees. We never considered wanting to leave the confines during the lunch break although I do not recall that anything prevented us doing so.

MARGARET'S MUSINGS

Margaret (née Flatt) Baxter

One of my earliest recollections was in form 1C. 'C' stood for County and all the girls in that class had come from homes beyond the Borough boundary. I met a friend whom I had not seen since Infant School days. I dropped my spectacle case in the aisle between our desks and she kindly picked it up for me. After that we became firm friends again.

Miss Moore was our first form mistress who taught us English, History and Scripture. With her large brown eyes, grey hair curled under at the sides and her measured voice she led us carefully and meticulously onward in our first year at grammar school.

Form 1 Alpha with their form teacher Miss Moore in 1948

Photograph courtesy of Derby Evening Telegraph

Our desks were spacious with a separate comfortable chair, which was real luxury after the wooden bench-type seat at Junior School. Here we could safely leave our spare books as we went to a different room for tuition in another subject. Nothing was missing on our return and the pin-ups inside the lid were undisturbed. In later years a friend put up a photograph of the boxer Freddy Mills! One of the staff did raise her eyebrows at that.

The headmistress in our early years was Miss Welbank. This lady, although small in stature, was formidable in discipline. One day when leaving a classroom, not looking where I was going, I collided with her. I managed to keep her upright while she bombarded me with questions. 'What is your name? Which class are you in? Where do you live? Where does your father work? I will have to get in touch with him about your behaviour.' I replied loftily, 'Oh, he doesn't work, he teaches!' I expect that remark went the rounds of the staffroom.

I found one of the most enjoyable classes was French with Miss Loydall. She was always a very cheerful, down to earth and fair teacher with whom I very nearly mastered French grammar!

As we moved up the school Miss Rhoda Newman and her music had a great influence on us. She was bright and vivacious and invariably kept our interest. One of the highlights was the preparation for Speech Day where our singing was a main feature. I still remember the occasion when international anthems were the theme for that year.

The winter of 1947 stands out because of the severe weather and lack of heating due to a coal shortage. We had to pile on as many clothes as possible. I remember we sat and wrote, for say fifteen minutes, and then were allowed to stand up and jump about, flapping our hands to get the circulation going before resuming work once more.

On the sports side I always enjoyed the swimming and even took part in one or two Galas. The stroke was usually freestyle and my efforts were certainly that! I would start off with front crawl and when I ran out of breath I resorted to breaststroke.

Needless to say I never came in first!

John Shakespeare's house in Stratford-upon-Avon, believed to be William Shakespeare's birthplace

Image Source: Wikipedia

The Sixth form was a pleasant two years when the staff became more human. Our chosen subjects were studied in depth and became more difficult to work at. Miss Helmore was a very understanding Head and gave us much encouragement. Our last summer term came all too quickly and after the final exams this period was spent in playing tennis, reading and helping out in the library, and making preparations for the sixth form revue. We also had various trips and one particular outing was a day at Stratford-upon-Avon to see *Much Ado about Nothing*. As I gave eight pages to it in my diary it must have made a great impression on me. Here it is as recorded over fifty years ago.

Saturday 10th June 1950

A visit to Stratford

Set off at 8.30 a.m. this morning complete with camera. Beetle and I sat together near the front of the bus with Tantor and Jally on the opposite side. Beautiful ride through Lichfield, Kenilworth and Warwick. There was not a drop of water across the road at the Kenilworth water splash. We arrived at Stratford at 11.30 a.m. We four betook ourselves to the river immediately and went on a motorboat called 'Delta'. There were numerous swans all round. The boat went up as far as the church and then turned and came down past the theatre and right under the two bridges. We went past beautiful houses with gardens sloping down to the river with their own private landing stages. This ride cost one shilling each. We passed Homer, Jenny, Bugsie, Sidge and Grace in a rowing boat.

On leaving the river we went to the church. There is a lovely avenue of trees leading up to the doors. Jally was holding forth about a white wedding. We had to pay sixpence to go in. Jally stayed outside and sketched. We saw where Shakespeare was baptized and the entry of his birth in the register. The windows are very beautiful. A girl was playing the organ while we were inside. We came out and walked round to the back of the church where it overlooks the river. Here we ate our lunch. Beetle sat with her legs over the wall, her feet dangling above the water. We quite thought she would lose her court shoes. We had a very tame chaffinch and sparrow. The chaffinch had very bright colours but the sparrow was short-sighted. He couldn't see the crumbs when we threw them straight at him. They both came quite near. I took three photos or rather Jally took one and I took two. Two were taken with the background of the river and one against a tree. I wanted to take one against the tombstones and call it Life and Death but they would not let me.

After leaving the church we wandered round the town a little and saw Shakespeare's house. We entered W. H. Smith's where I bought a painted pot for Mum and one or two postcards, while Tantor bought a Shakespeare birthday book, and a small edition of *Much Ado*.

We reached the theatre at 2.15 p.m. and bought a programme and a large book of photographs. Beetle and I had to sub on Tantor for that. I'm absolutely broke. I don't think I shall be able to go to school for the rest of the month. The theatre was beautiful. As we went to the left for the dress circle, there was a small pool with a rock fountain, which kept the air deliciously cool. In the window on the staircase, there are small statuette figures of Hamlet, Falstaff and Prince Hal, etc. We were on the back row of the dress circle and had a superb view. The seats were very comfortable.

Much Ado about Nothing was delightful, with John Gielgud as Benedick and Peggy Ashcroft as Beatrice. The costumes were bright and gay and the scenery just wonderful and so cleverly made. The play opened with a garden background. There were two sorts of brick arbours with statues inside. In between, the two arbours were three steps with a countryside scene behind.

John Gielgud and Peggy Ashcroft as Benedict and Beatrice in Gielgud's production of *Much Ado About Nothing* at the Shakespeare Memorial Theatre, Stratford-upon-Avon, *c.*1950. Photograph by Angus McBean

Now when an inside banqueting hall was needed these arbours opened out to form the walls of an ornate room and two doors closed at the back to shut out the back scenery. The statues remained. Lights were brought in. I thought it was marvellous the way it was all done. This scene shifting was done by servants dressed in pink and yellow livery and some in pink and black. In the second act it was even more wonderful. The scene opened with a kind of platform on columns, with more columns in the background. Upon this platform sat Benedick shaving while Claudio and Don Pedro talked up to him.

When the scene changed again these columns moved back on wheels, the platform sliding in as it moved to reveal a public hall behind, placed at an angle to the centre of the stage. This was for the Dogberry and Verges night-watch scene. When a church was needed for the marriage scene these columns wheeled left and right to show the interior of a church. The people entered through the columns from the left. These were the most spectacular scene changes. The play ended about 5.15 p.m. We went onto the balcony overlooking the river during the second interval.

When we left the theatre we wandered round looking for a milk bar, where Tantor, Beetle and I had a milkshake and Jally had a cup of tea. My hayfever was attacking me again. We had tea on the grass in front of the theatre. Tantor and I went to look for a drinking fountain. We found one later but it was a silly contrivance. One had to push a button hard and the water squirted out in a long curve-wetting everything within reach including Beetle and myself. The idea was to catch some water in one's cup if it was possible to get it in a correct position!

While we were engaged in this Miss Graham and Miss Robinson came along to watch and Graham said, 'Don't be more than half an hour will you?' By then it was 6.25 p.m. and we had to leave soon after 6.30 p.m. Miss Newman also came along and had a good laugh. We caused some amusement all round.

We returned home the same way as we came and we still kept the sunroof open. Reached home about 9.10 p.m. It was a Wheildons Castle Donington bus so he brought us to Alvaston – Seago, Homer and myself. Mr Wheildon himself had taken us. The buses are beautifully comfy. It had been a truly wonderful day.

Another contribution was written in the summer of 1948 whilst under the influence of the rhythm of G. K. Chesterton's 'Lepanto'. Some of us had cricket fever due to the visit of the Australian touring team led by the legendary Don Bradman, and were inspired to produce the following pastiche:

Bradman with his Wm. Sykes bat, in the early 1930s

Image Source: Wikipedia

Cricket Lepanto

White pants gleaming at the Oval in the sun,

And the Captain of Australia is grinning as they run;

There's laughter of the devil in that face of England feared,

And it stirs the aged wrinkles 'cause he hasn't got a beard,

It curls the blood-red crescent, the crescent of his lips,

For the strongest knees of England are shaking in the slips.

They have dared the Worcester bowlers with their batting wild and free,

They have crushed the Leicester batsmen singing 'merry men are we'.

Yardley has cast his arms abroad for England to be boss,

And called the county captains not to stand a loss.

The cold skies of England are drizzling on the grass;

And the anxious crowds are swaying in a damp and dripping mass;

From cricket grounds fantastical ring fain the English groans,

And the Aussies in their triumph are laughing at the moans.

Dull cheers rising from the fans half heard,

Where only in an English pav. a cricket king has stirred,

Where risen from a backwood home in that dry far-off land,

The strong arm of the Aussies takes weapons from the stand.

The great and mighty warrior to whom the cuckoo sang

When first he set intrepid foot upon our changeful land.

In that enormous silence, tiny and unafraid,

Comes out across the cricket pitch, the bravest of the brave.

Strong bats cracking as the ball hits hard,

Don Bradman of Australia is throwing down his card.

Stiff flags straining in the cold wind-blast,

And lots of little fielders are running very fast.

Sunlight gleaming on the ball twixt Yardley's thumbs,

Then the cheering, then the groaning, then the tea-bell and he comes.

D.B. laughing with his bat in hand.

Squaring of his shoulders as he takes the wicket stand,

Holding of his head up, confident and sure.

Bright hope of Aussies, Ha!

Great fear of England, Bah!

Don Bradman of Australia

Is batting here once more.

W.G. is in his paradise above the evening star,

(Don Bradman of Australia is hitting fast and far.)

Where are green and velvet pitches and skies that always please,

A heaven that is only reached via stiffened arms and knees.

He shakes the cricket pitches as he rises from his ease

And he strides among the tree-tops and is taller than the trees,

And his voice through all the pitches is a thunder sent to bring

George Griffith and old Wilsher and Grundy on the wing.

Giants and the Genii,

Sure and quick of foot and eye,

Whose strong- armed batting hit the sky

When Alfred Mynn was king.

They rush in cricket flannels from the red clouds of the mom,

By temples where the football Gods shut up their eyes in scorn;

They rise in white shirts roaring from the green hells of the sea

Where broken bats and bashed in balls and wonky wickets be;

On them the woodworms saunter, and on them green lichens curl,

Splashed with a splendid colour, the colour of the pearl;

They come in mighty armies from their haunts in many a place,

They gather and they wonder and give worship to old Grace.

And he saith 'Break down the batsmen where Aussie strength doth lie.

And stop them hitting English balls so pert and freshly spry,

And chase their bowlers, flying day and night keep up the pace.

For that which was our trouble comes again of southern race'.

We have set the seal of Britain on all things under sun,

Of knowledge and of sorrow and endurance of things done;

But a noise is on the pitches, on the pitches and I know

The voice that shook our palaces ten long, long years ago;

It is he that saith not 'Kismet'; it is he that knows not Fate;

It is Lindwall, it is Miller, it is Harvey in the gate!

It is he whose loss is laughter when he counts the wager worth:

Put down your bats upon him, that our balls be on the turf.

For he heard crowds groaning and he heard bats jar

(DB. of Australia is going out to war).

Sudden and still Hurrah!

Bolt from 'Down Under'. Ha!

DB. of Australia is come from afar.

Yardley is on his wild-moors in the rough roads of the north

(DB. of Australia is girt and going forth)

Where the grey skies splutter and the white clouds shift

And the farm-folk labour and the pitchforks lift.

He swings his bat of willow and he claps his hands of stone;

The noise is gone through counties all; the noise is gone alone;

The land is full of tangled things and texts of aching eyes

And dead is all the innocence of anger and surprise,

And batsman batteth batsman in a narrow dusty place,

And bowler dreads the ball that hath a new and ghastly face,

And gulley hateth long on that Brown played in Leicestershire

But D.B. of Australia, he has no time for fear.

D.B. calling through the blast and the eclipse

Crying with the trumpet, the trumpet of his lips.

Trumpet that sayeth, Ha!

Cricketo Gloria!

D.B. of Australia

Is shouting in the slips.

Oh Jackson's in his backroom with the Aussies on his chest

(DB. of Australia is hitting out his best.)

The walls are hung with press cuts and old flannels worn and thin,

And doughty men creep out of it and doughty men creep in.

He holds a crystal phial that has colours like the moon,

He touches and it tingles, and he trembles very soon,

And his face is as a fungus of a leprous white and grey,

Like plants in the high houses that are shuttered from the day,

And death is in the phial and the end of noble strain,

But Don Bradman of Australia is batting hard again.

D.B's hitting and his balls have whirled

Where the crowds are roaring and the flag is furled

Four upon four. Ha! Ha!

Six upon six, hurrah!

DB. of Australia

His mighty arm hath hurled.

Yardley was in his dressing room before the battle broke

(DB. of Australia has whammed a mighty stroke),

The famous room where years ago Grace, Pilch and all the rest

Prepared to fight for England's might and fight their very best.

He sees the smooth-rolled pitch like a monstrous sunlit sea,

Where wickets glint in morning sun a ghostly vengeful three,

They fling great shadows forwards, making crease and grasses dark,

They veil the golden sunlight and paint the whole ground stark.

And above the ground the swallows swoop in happy, carefree flight,

And around the ground are crowds who have witnessed many a fight.

English watchers sick and anxious, all a labouring race repines

Like a race in sunken cities, like a nation in the mines.

They talk of English batsmen and of bowlers such as Wright

And wistfully think of far-off days when British hopes were bright.

They are countless, voiceless, hopeless as those fallen or fleeing on

Before the high King's horses in the granite of Babylon.

And many a batsman sickens in his quiet room in hell

When a vanquished face looks inward through the lattice of his cell,

And his cricket God's forgotten when that glum face inward peers

But DB. of Australia

He scorns these waiting fears.

D. B. pounding down the steps to that white gate,

Ambling to the wicket stand in easy carefree state;

Swiping to the boundary, and snicking through the slips,

Adding yet another run, with laughter on his lips,

Knocking up of centuries with sure and easy slashes,

All towards the final goal, of taking home the Ashes.

Vivat Englandia!

Cricketo Gloria!

But D.B. of Australia

Has crushed all with his bashes.

Oh Compton in his glory sets the bat back in the stand.

(D.B. of Australia rides homeward with a band.)

He sees along a dusty road a straggling youthful crowd,

And well he knows their object and though famous he's not proud.

And he grins a wide and cheery grin, and laughing takes the pen,

But D.B. of Australia is southward bound again.

Margaret Baxter (nee Flatt) et al.

JUNE'S JOTTINGS

June Allen

NON
SINE PULVERE
PALMA

In September 1943, as a new girl at Homelands, I knew of the great events of the war but was touched by them at only a very personal level.

The official school uniform list was worrying. All clothing was rationed and cloth of poor quality. Wages were low for my father. My gym slip was made by mother at a 'Mend-and-Make-Do' evening class held in the Junior School. I stood on a desk to have the very deep hem pinned up. Everything was geared for long wear and future growth. The three box pleats (front and back) all overlapped. No need! By 1948 my bust didn't cause a bulge. There were such generous overlaps at the shoulders that it was twelve months before the buttons were moved and the knot of my tie saw light above the yoke.

Mother had the feeling it was patriotic to make clothes at home. My blouses were made from fabric from a stall in the open market. There was no white cotton and they had to be 'a nice shade of biscuit'. I was coaxed into being different from the other girls by the implication that white blouses were 'common'.

On that first morning we sat on the parquet floor of the lovely school hall waiting to be assigned to our forms. Beside me was a girl in a navy and white spotted cotton dress. She explained to the teacher, defensively, that her father was in the army and that her mother could not afford the uniform. I'm sure the school helped her over this. Certainly, gym shoes were on loan from the games store.

Nothing I wore was quite standard. My indoor shoes were nurses' ward shoes with the rubber heels cut (uncomfortably) low. My knickers were sky-blue instead of regulation navy. My P.T. vest was a (boy!!) cousin's hand-me-down and had a navy neckband and cuffs. Thanks to a kind neighbour with older girls, my happiest item was a summer dress of pre-war style uniform. It was a lighter blue than the current butcher-blue button-through dresses. It had kick pleats at the hem and a double row of tiny pearl buttons at the front neck. Velour hats and fabric scarves were replaced by blue berets and an ingenious hand-knitted scarf. Diagonal stripes of sky-blue and navy were produced by constantly increasing the stitches at one side and decreasing them at the other.

Later in the war, navy blazers gave place to mid-blue with a pocket badge that included the motto 'Non Sine Pulvere Palma'.

No Palms Without Dust

Since the wartime cloth rapidly lost its nap, we translated the Latin as, 'If you haven't got a duster, use this'.

By 1943, the long underground air-raid shelters above the top playing field were not used, although there was a short-lived 'Dig for Victory' campaign in the form of vegetable plots on the air-raid shelter mounds and in the garden east of Homelands House. We tended them in house-groups and I remember demonstrating how carrots were thinned. South of the house, above the netball courts, were blackcurrant and gooseberry bushes. We were sent to pick these for Miss Ure to preserve for school dinners.

In the dining room, wartime food had to include boiled beetroot as a hot vegetable, 'Pom' dried potato-mash, 'snoek' whale meat and, often, 'Spam' canned meat. Mushy peas were a staple. We were glad of our meals.

Fuel became short. Homework was impossible where a large family shared the one heated living room. Late Prep was instituted so that we could work in the fading heat of the classroom after hours. Late Prep teas were nicely served in the dining room beforehand. They gave us cocoa and fish paste rolls. We felt this was no hardship but enjoyed it.

Able-bodied teachers were often doing war work and retired members of staff came back to help at Homelands. Three had taught my mother during the First World War, when the school had been the Central School for Girls in Hastings Street. They were: Miss Mary Witt (English), Miss Pakeman (Mathematics) and Miss Yates (French).

Younger staff were on a fire-watching rota. They slept on canvas camp beds in the staffroom and at intervals patrolled the corridors to look for incendiary bombs. Fire-buckets, stirrup pump and a long-handled shovel were on hand below each staircase. Two brave souls had a fright: groping their way with shaded torches in the blackout, they saw a distant red glow, but it was only a red-shaded lantern left burning by mistake!

In the grim, dark war years the staff gave us treats that families could not always provide. The First-years were taken to see *Peter Pan* at the Grand Theatre, and the whole school to see the film *Henry V*. There were school plays, Christmas form parties, lectures (who was the LEA officer who spoke of his Everest expedition?) and grand speech days.

As the war ended, we sang the National Anthems of all the Allies at Speech Day and there was soon a visit from a party of French girls who toured Derbyshire with us.

JOYCE'S JOURNAL

Joyce (née Mercer) Varty

I remember my first day at Homelands very well indeed. It was a wet Monday, and only the first year pupils were there, so that the huge building (my junior school was a collection of wooden huts) seemed silent and empty. The cloakroom and corridors were dark, rather gloomy and smelt of polish, but the curious, yellow stone staircase, each step edged with a narrow pattern in black and white, was more cheerful, and the upper form room, with its large windows overlooking the playing fields, gave a distant view of Sinfin Moor, near which I lived – a comforting sight.

Photograph courtesy of Marjorie Calow

Miss Moore, the form teacher, spoke softly (I never did hear her shout) but she had authority, despite her strange hairstyle, which included a little sausage-shaped curl over each ear. She taught Ancient History, English and Scripture to her form, and was known as 'Jeremiah the sorrowful prophet'. She was always grave, and was not even much amused when, in answer to her question about what the ancient Egyptians did with the innards of the mummies they were preparing, Sally Cooper said, very confidently, 'They pickled them, Miss Moore!'. On our first morning she gave out exercise books (to be taken home and covered neatly with brown paper), wooden rulers, rubbers, pencils and tubular metal pens with broad nibs that spat ink in wrong places regularly. (Fountain pens were not allowed.)

I thought the individual desks with lots of storage space were wonderful. Junior school had only provided iron-framed double desks with sloping wooden lids over narrow shelves, from which everything regularly fell onto the floor. Oddly, the 'blackboard' was yellow, written on with blue chalk. There was nothing racist behind this: it was said to be easier on the eyes! Outside, the grounds were marvellous.

102

There were even horse chestnut trees, and conkers for the taking!

When real work began, the next day, we had our first visit to the Chemistry lab. with its long benches, high stools, sinks, gas taps and pervasive smells. In strong contrast to later days, we begged Miss Steel, the Science mistress, to give us some homework! It was a novelty then. The first French lesson with Miss Loydall was great fun, as she drew pictures on the board of the objects whose names we had to learn. 'Voici la pipe' really came to life!

As time passed, the school became familiar ground: the geography room, presided over by Miss Jones, with its vast desks to accommodate large maps and atlases, the beautiful library (a haven of peace), the well-lit Art room, the hall (complete with stage and balcony) where before Assembly the high windows were opened by a tall girl with an even taller pole, and the well-equipped gym – rib-stalls, ropes, vaulting horse and all.

I wasn't an over-enthusiastic gymnast, on the whole. It was an awful fag to change and change back, all in forty-five minutes, and I always managed to evade the bothersome showers we were supposed to take after each session. It took too long to get dry, dressed, and on to the following lesson in time. This nuisance often happened on Friday afternoons when I was in either year 4 or 5, and the English lesson, which followed almost always suffered a ragged start. Miss Witt, who was guiding us through Macbeth at the time, was very patient, and usually waited for everyone to arrive, but one day she decided to begin on time, and greeted us with, 'Good afternoon, half-class'. Quick as a flash, Shirley Briggs called out, 'Good afternoon, half-wit!'. To her eternal credit, Miss Witt laughed with the rest of us.

I can't remember many of the floor exercises we did in P.E. but one which Miss Land always trotted out after Christmas (she said it was to get rid of the plum pudding) involved kneeling on all fours and repeatedly stretching forward until our noses touched the floor. This contortion rejoiced in the name of 'Pluto Shifts', Pluto being, I suppose, a dog. Work on the apparatus was more interesting, and, one glorious day, we were taught to climb up the ropes. Practising this new skill on the bus stop at hometime, I was, unfortunately, caught at the top by a passing prefect. It cost me a house point. We played games; netball and hockey in winter, and tennis and rounders in summer. For tennis we walked in crocodile to Normanton Rec. I liked rounders best, but was always sorry we never played cricket. At Reginald Street baths, among floating detritus, we were taught to swim. In the fond hope of turning us all into ladies, they tried to teach us ballroom dancing, too, and this was included as part of the programme for the form Christmas parties held in the hall.

Needlework was not my favourite lesson. It seemed such a waste of time to be doing what could be done at home when there were so many interesting things to learn in 'proper lessons'! I had similar feelings about Domestic Science, for which we had to bring from home a basket of ingredients and cooking dishes, and trail along the covered way to Homelands House, which always smelled of fish pie, cheese and disinfectant. I opted out of both these experiences as soon as it was possible.

Chemistry teacher Miss Lavelle with her nephew at the summer fete *c.*1957.

Photograph courtesy of Margaret Page (Left)

The 'covered way' to Homelands House

Photograph courtesy of Derby Evening Telegraph (Right)

Music was quite well taught, I think. We did a bit of theory, listened to records and learned a variety of songs. I hated having to sing solo in the first term, when Miss Newman was looking for new choir members. It was a real, and dreaded, ordeal, but I liked the songs and carols we learned as a class. These were often used on Speech Days, and I remember one distinguished visitor on the platform saying, 'I have never heard girls sing so beautiful!' For one Speech Day we learned all the National Anthems of the countries 'on our side' in the War – and fine tunes they were. At least once, we had a carol service in St. Giles's Church, near the school.

The War had quite an effect on our education. We 'dug for victory' on the humps over the air-raid shelters just outside the windows. I grew 'lettuces with Miss Loydall' and helped to harvest blackcurrants. On two Saturdays we went out to a farm near Shottle and walked up and down the long field putting artificial fertiliser on every individual plant in the crop by hand. I suppose fertiliser must have been rationed too! There was a barrage balloon on the front lawn and Italian prisoners of war in the house next to the school. Perhaps it was their presence which caused our spinney, next to their garden, to be designated 'out of bounds'! Even though actual hostilities finished at the end of our second year, it was a very long time before austerities ended and life returned to normal. During the endlessly hard winter of 1946–47 I remember struggling to school past teams of German prisoners hacking ice, several inches thick, off the roads.

The War also curtailed school trips. It was a real event to be out of school during school hours! Red letter days were marked by a visit to the Cavendish Cinema (we walked there, in crocodile, as usual) to see Olivier's *Henry V*, an afternoon trip to see the Derby Shakespeare Theatre Company perform *Romeo and Juliet* at the Railway Institute (miraculously, we didn't walk there!) and coach outings to Haddon Hall and Chatsworth House. At Chatsworth, the guide turned on the copper willow tree fountain and gave us all a good sprinkling!

Cavendish Cinema in early 1938

Photograph courtesy of Cinema Treasures

We were never exposed to the dangers of drugs, but I'm sure we were far too sensible to ever consider harming ourselves, anyway, and the threat of air-raids provided quite enough excitement to set the adrenalin running. Neither did we have the cash to waste of today's teenagers. However, the turbulent years didn't pass us by entirely, and I remember, with shame, some of the troubles we caused certain teachers.

One, Miss Wilson, came to teach us history as a temporary supply when our regular teacher, Miss Jewsbury, left to take up a headship. Poor Miss Wilson had earned the nickname 'Old Juicy' when teaching (temporarily) at Bemrose School, because she was always saying, 'do you see' after explaining a point. She struggled with us, too, and once, when she asked how we thought Napoleon got away after the Battle of the Nile, some bright spark called out, 'He swam'! On another occasion, when we had to take turns to read aloud from a textbook, I pretended to have difficulty, stumbling over every other word. The dear old soul said nothing, but when I came to a word with more than half a dozen letters, read it out for me herself. It was a very different matter when Mrs Wignall arrived. We had to do two years' work in one, to cover the syllabus before School Certificate, and she paced to and fro like a caged lion at the front of the class, barking out reams of notes, which we wrote down furiously until our wrists ached.

Another victim of our disruptive humour was Miss Neale, who taught Science. It was Chemistry when most of the trouble flared up. If only it had been taught in the light of modern atomic theory, it would have been fascinating and understandable. As it was, it was too much like Domestic Science just learning 'recipes' by rote, and seeing that they worked in experiments. The show needed livening up. Small, round Miss Neale in her white lab. coat was dubbed 'The Snowball', and it's a wonder we didn't drive her to despair. It was fun to bombard her with quirky questions (I once asked why rheumatic joints ached when it rained) just to hear her say, 'I haven't got the answer to that at my fingertips. I'm a chemist'. Sometimes the worst rebels were shut in the Preparation Room at the back of the Lab, and on one occasion I remember Shirley Briggs, a very clever girl who later won an Exhibition in History to Royal Holloway College, being the occupant. Her voice cut through the glass door, singing, 'What shall we do with the science teacher ... Tickle her toes with a Bunsen burner ... Pickle her in acid till she decomposes', and similar scurrilous lines to the tune of 'The Drunken Sailor'. It really was a miracle that any of us got through the General Science exam.

There was no tomfoolery in Miss Robinson's French class: her sharp tongue saw to that. Neither would our form mistress at the time, Miss Graham, stand any nonsense. How I wish she had taught me Mathematics. It would have saved me much strife in later life, and I would never have dared to give her 'the black spot' as I did to kind, young Miss Hancock, who did her best to keep me applied to the subject in hand. (I was reading *Treasure Island* at the time, and found it much more interesting than figures.)

Despite all this mayhem in class, discipline was, in fact, good in the school. There was no running in the corridors, and if anyone ever was so careless as to run, with only one foot, near Miss Yates's door, she was sure to shoot out with a beckoning finger, and say, in a loud, hollow voice, 'My room, at four', where French exercises would await the culprit. House points could be lost for misbehaviour, and the wrath of the house captain would fall upon the miscreant's head. House points could, of course, also be gained for good work, and during my first two years, when Miss Welbank was the much-respected headmistress, she saw every piece of work which earned a point, and initialled it herself. I can remember queuing many a lunchtime in the corridor outside her study, to get my point awarded.

I have many happy memories of Homelands, where we were given such a wonderful, sound, all-round education, for which I shall always be grateful.

STELLA'S SECRETS

Stella (née Clarricoats) Allen

In July 1943 I left a school built towards the end of the nineteenth century to go to a relatively new building that smelt of polish, new furniture and new exercise books. I was very impressed by Homelands.

The nightmare of showers after gym stays with me. Being an only child, no-one had seen me naked except my Mum. Perhaps taking my clothes off publicly was made more horrendous by the fact that I was, at eleven and twelve, completely flat-chested! I still wore a liberty bodice, whilst all the other girls had a bra! All my misery was watched over by the frightening Miss Land.

In 1945, as the war ended, we learned the National Anthems of our Allies. I'm not sure why this should be memorable, but perhaps it's because I can still remember the words and tunes of most of them. Mathematics was such a sad mystery to me even though I surprisingly, against all predictions to the contrary, passed Mathematics in the School Certificate. My needlework took me ages to complete and always ended up grubby, with too tight stitching. We made 'useful' things like a cookery apron and a needlework apron (why did we need an apron for sewing?), a cross-stitch serviette ring and – joy of joy – a pair of big, blue school knickers! I never actually wore them as they were obviously made for a deformed person: who could walk with the gusset sewn in east-west instead of north-south? Mother was cross about this I remember, as she had paid good money and some clothing coupons to acquire this useless garment.

My surname has been 'Allen' for the last forty-one years. How gratefully I accepted that short name, having laboured all my school life with 'Clarricoats': imagine the grief and sweat caused embroidering my name on a shoe-bag, particularly when the Wretched girl next to me was surnamed 'Foy'! I hope she married someone with an eleven-letter name to compensate.

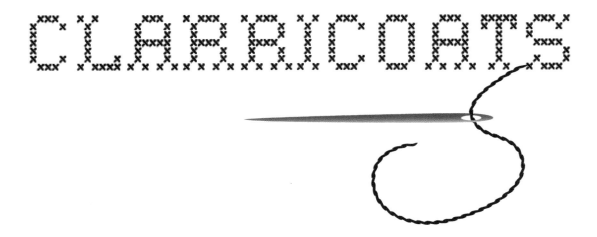

MARJORIE'S MISCELLANY – Part II

Marjorie Calow

'The past is a foreign country; they do things differently there ...'

The situation in the teaching profession in 1953 was very different from that in the twenty-first century. Some time during my final term at college Miss Helmore telephoned me, told me that Miss Neale was leaving and asked if I'd like to join the staff as Chemistry Mistress. I have absolutely no recollection of being interviewed or filling in an application form; the whole process just seemed to proceed smoothly until I found myself duly appointed. I had no postgraduate teaching qualification and only a third-class degree (albeit in Special Chemistry), but at that time female chemists were as rare as hens' teeth. In fact, as Chemistry graduates, we all (male <u>and</u> female) felt that the world was at our feet. Looking back, I find it amazing that I had no qualms about taking on such a responsible job (including teaching sixth-formers only three years younger than myself and being responsible for the work of two laboratory assistants) at the age of twenty-one. I just got on with it and quite enjoyed it. Certainly I had no problems in maintaining discipline. My main problems were boredom with the marking (I remember one evening spent marking ninety accounts of how to separate salt from sand) and the stress (as it would now be designated!) of having to cope with examinations, reports and Christmas parties at the end of the Christmas term, while at the same time attempting (not very successfully) to be a dutiful wife and daughter.

I <u>do</u> remember feeling a sense of elation during my first staff meeting, which was held in the library on a sunny day in September, immediately before term started. The feeling was: 'Gosh! Here am I, a real live grammar school mistress!'. A number of new teachers started that term. We were all much the same age, although the arts graduates, who would have done a teaching qualification, must have been a year or so older than I was. Some of us were 'young marrieds'; I got married in the December after I returned to Homelands in September and was very proud to return after Christmas wearing a wedding ring and instructing everyone to address me by my married name.

Mrs. M. Harrison.

Joan Smith taught Physics (she was a brilliant teacher – much better than I was) and for a short time we and our respective spouses were friendly outside school hours. Barbara Lacey taught English and was married to a clergyman. Years later, our paths crossed again when we both worked for the Workers' Educational Association, she as a part-time tutor in Nottingham and myself as a full-time employee in Derby. Janet Burbage, who taught French, was also married. The remaining members of the new intake were all single at that time. Mary Wilson taught Latin and Kathleen Kemp taught – was it French or Mathematics? The only one of these colleagues with whom I have remained in contact (although I can see all their faces and the way they walked and talked to this day) was Audrey Thompson, who taught Geography. She eventually married a doctor from Boots, where my husband also worked. In the strange way that coincidences happen, I discovered recently that Audrey's husband was later connected with the hospital where my ex-husband's second wife works as a consultant. Audrey had four children and recently sent me a photograph of the whole family. She did not look at all like the Audrey I remember so clearly.

It was, of course, strange to be on the staff as a colleague, with people who had formerly taught me. They were a wonderful bunch of dedicated women. I remember once chatting to Celia Hughes while we were washing our hands in the cloakroom. She was bemoaning the fact that the facilities were inadequate for 'some thirty-odd women', adding 'some of them very odd'. When Celia retired and her aged parents had died I was told that she 'swung a loose leg' (meaning that she travelled a lot). This information, like much other information about the staff, came from Grace Graham and Kathleen Robinson. A whole book could be written about this delightful, devoted pair. Their friendship dated from 1946, when they met on the day of their interviews (successful, as it turned out) for their respective posts. Both of them rushed to the railway station afterwards, in order to be back at their schools the next day, and each respected the other for this manifestation of rectitude. As senior mistresses, they were amongst the highest paid teachers in Derby; they volunteered this information to me many years later. When they took up their posts, Grace lodged with Miss Haslam in Duffield Road; Kathleen lodged at The Vicarage in Normanton until her parents came to join her in Derby. After Kathleen's parents died, Grace and Kathleen moved to 190 Warwick Avenue, which became the venue for a variety of happy occasions.

190 Warwick Avenue, Derby

Images courtesy of K S Dhindsa © 2016

This house was of a solid, detached, three bedroomed design, built (I imagine) in the 1930s. It was always immaculately maintained structurally and kept as neat as a pin by a faithful 'daily', whose daughter took on the same role when her mother retired. Although the house itself was lovely, it was the renowned hospitality of Grace and Kathleen that made its atmosphere so wonderful. Grace was a fabulous cook and her talent was complemented by Kathleen's organisational skills. Since neither of them could bear the thought of Homelands going comprehensive, they both retired slightly early and began a busy and pleasurable phase of their lives which lasted many years. Their gastronomic and other domestic skills dovetailed neatly with their hobbies. If you wanted to know the best place to eat (or, for that matter, to stay) in Stratford-upon-Avon, they could tell you, since they attended the Royal Shakespeare Theatre regularly, sometimes staying in Stratford for a whole week so that they could see all the plays in which they were interested.

Trips to France were an annual event and, of course, Kathleen's fluent French was invaluable on these expeditions. Grace drove the car and Kathleen navigated. They returned with the boot full of French wines and cheeses. They once told me, to my horror, that they never declared the litre of absolute alcohol they always purchased to make cassis, not realising that such a declaration was mandatory. (As a working chemist, I was used to accounting for every drop of absolute alcohol.) The thought of two innocent little old ladies getting away with this is quite amusing. In this country, they regularly went to Warwickshire to pick fruit; wherever they went they were well-known and popular (a place was always saved for them in the car park outside the theatre at Stratford). The fruit was duly transformed by Grace into delicious jam. She also made marmalade, which was eagerly snapped up by the cognoscenti at the coffee mornings held at their home in May every year, when vast sums were raised for Christian Aid and Cancer Research. The various stalls were looked after by past and present members of staff and other friends and the event was well patronised by people from their wide circle of acquaintances.

Other events that took place at Warwick Avenue included meetings of the Homelands Old Students' Association. For a number of years, Grace and Kathleen attended a theology class at St. Helen's House, where I worked as a Tutor Organiser. The class always had a wonderful party, with lots of delicious food and drink, at the end of term and I was privileged to attend a couple of these. At a more personal level, I was invited to many meals with Grace and Kathleen over the years, both when I was living in Nottingham and when I was living in Melbourne. Most memorable were the meals on a day usually just before Christmas Eve. They had a great line in apéritifs (an 'Americano' a lethal mixture of Campari and Extra Dry Martini – was one of their favourites) and I would be handed one of these on arrival. There was wine French, of course with the meal. Kathleen would have laid the table with festive decorations beforehand. The meal would start with Grace's special soup, served with a dollop of cream. This was followed by turkey (selected and collected from a farm run by an old girl) with all the trimmings. Next came a selection of French cheeses and then Grace's home-made Christmas pudding, served with brandy butter. We finished with petits fours, coffee and liqueurs ... Those meals were the highlight of my Christmas. Grace and Kathleen were devout Christians and worked hard at the Cathedral. Together they did the flowers on many occasions. Grace did embroidery and Kathleen looked after the Cathedral Library for many years. In my recollections of this wonderful couple I have concentrated on their long and happy retirement.

The end is rarely good for any of us, so I will end this section of my narrative on that up-beat note.

In fact, my account of my return as a teacher has been somewhat dominated by this section. This is because some of the information I gleaned from Grace and Kathleen after we had all left Homelands for good has been incorporated in the earlier sections of my memories. All that remains to be said about the time when I returned (which lasted from September 1953 to April 1956) is to mention a few of the pupils I taught. Inevitably, perhaps, I remember only the girls I taught in the sixth form. Of these, I kept in touch with two for a few years, but then failed to maintain the contact. I have no idea why I lost contact with these two, but I do regret the loss.

As I get older I find myself thinking more and more frequently: 'I wonder what became of ... [whoever]'. This applies particularly to people I met at college and people I met at Boots.) Christine Tong became a doctor and the last I heard of her she was working as a GP in Sutton Coldfield. Gwendoline Fawkes was a biologist and worked I think for the Blood Transfusion Service in Manchester. But even that memory is uncertain. I remember also Celia Key and Cynthia Wozencroft and a Welsh girl with a Welsh name beginning with 'M'. And that is all. It would be pleasant to think that I had some influence on and am remembered by a few of the girls I taught, just as I was influenced by several of the wonderful women who taught me but who knows? One thing is certain: the education I received at Homelands Grammar School for Girls was the best education any girl of my generation and class could have hoped for.

(I left Homelands in 1956 and followed my husband to Boots. He was put on a graduate training scheme and eventually became Head of Patents. I worked for three years as a practical analytical chemist and then as a technical information officer, writing material for the firm's contributions to the British Pharmacopoeia, the British Pharmaceutical Codex and various government bodies. After twenty-two years of Suspended Animation, I forsook joyfully both chemistry and matrimony – but that is not part of the Homelands story.)

Prefects
Homelands Grammar School
Derby

May 1949

May 1950

Photographs courtesy of Marjorie Calow

112

Party at Melbourne, Saturday 8 September 1951
Back Row: June, Marjorie, Margaret, Pat
Front row: Joyce, Stella, Dorothy

Party at Quarndon, fifty years later,
Thursday 13 December 2001
(Pat was absent on Jury Service)

Photographs courtesy of Marjorie Calow

Tributes paid to a 'devoted' teacher

Friends to say farewell to 'a true inspiration'

FRIENDS of a former Derby teacher who was 'absolutely devoted to her pupils' are expected to attend her funeral service at Derby Cathedral tomorrow.

Kathleen Robinson died peacefully, aged 89, on January 31 after a long career.

Miss Robinson was well-known for her characteristically stern but passionate teaching at the former Homelands Grammar School for Girls, now the site of Village School in Normanton, from the 1940s to the 1970s.

'She was quite simply one of the most professional people that I have ever met,' former colleague Cynthia Marks, of Duffield Road, Allestree, said. 'Teaching was her life she was absolutely devoted to her pupils. They just don't make them like Kathleen any more.'

Miss Robinson's teaching career in the city began in 1945 when she was given the post of head of modern languages at Homelands Grammar School for Girls.

A formidable disciplinarian, she also encouraged her pupils with extra-curricular activities such as amateur theatrical productions.

'She had been a French scholar at Royal Holloway and Bedford College at the University of London before coming to Derby,' Mrs Marks explained. 'Her academic prowess was well known. But she was also a true educator, whose constant aim was to widen the horizons of those she taught.'

In 1948, she arranged the first post-war exchange visits between Homelands girls and girls in France.

Jennifer Joyce (57), of Hindscarth Crescent, Mickleover, was a pupil at the school from 1955 to 1962.

She said: 'Miss Robinson was a wonderful teacher who always managed to bring the best out of us. She was a true inspiration and this was proven by the fact that I went on to return to the school in 1970 to teach.'

Throughout the end of the 1940s and in the 1950s, her theatrical productions became more and mere elaborate.

Mrs Marks said: 'She was an indefatigable producer – tirelessly encouraging her young actors to give as professional a performance as they could.'

Canon David Truby, of Derby Cathedral, said: 'She was a very gentle woman with a self-effacing humour who will be sadly missed.'

Derby Evening Telegraph – Tuesday 12th February 2002 by David Clensy

A French Play produced by Kathleen Robinson
(Lower VI & Upper VI)

Photographs courtesy of Marjorie Calow

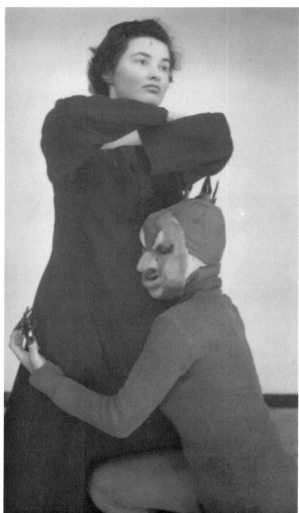

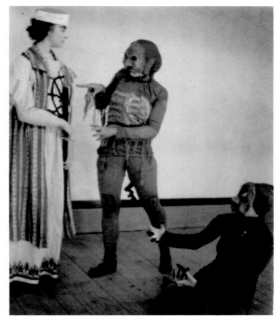

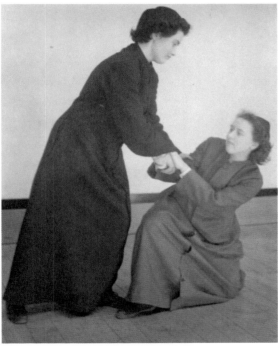

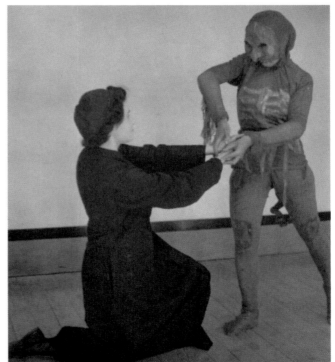

A hard double act to follow

THE death of Kathleen Robinson on January 31, in her 90th year, will have evoked countless memories for many people in Derby.

Miss Robinson was head of modern languages at Homelands Grammar School for Girls from 1945 until her retirement in 1973 and tribute has already been made in the Derby Evening Telegraph (February 17) to her high academic standards, her devotion to her students and her school drama productions.

As the memories flood back, I realise how impossible it is to speak of Kathleen without mentioning her friend and colleague Miss Grace Graham, head of the mathematics department. They were a team. For more than 30 years they shared a home and had many interests in common, drama being one. Kathleen produced the school plays and Grace designed and made the costumes.

Photograph courtesy of Marjorie Calow

Outside school, in the 1950s and 1960s, they both belonged to the Religious Drama Guild, performing plays in Derby Cathedral, St Luke's, St Werburgh's and other churches in the diocese.

At the same time they belonged to the Derby Grammar Schools Staffs Dramatic Society which gave public performances annually. They were regular theatre-goers locally and frequent visitors to Stratford upon-Avon.

Both were members of the Cathedral and Bridge Chapel congregations and, for some 25 years following their retirement, they catalogued and cared for the Cathedral library, only relinquishing the task when climbing to reach the upper shelves became too hazardous an undertaking.

They loved books and reading, needlework, music, cooking and travel, especially in France which they would tour by car, calling en route on their many French friends, some of whom had been French assistants at school and who had remained friends for life.

They had some good friends in a winegrowing area from where they brought adequate supplies to entertain their Derby friends in the ensuing year!

For those who knew Kathleen and Grace, their annual charity coffee morning was a social 'must' and over the ears they raised substantial amounts or Christian Aid and Cancer Research.

Their hospitality was legendary and their links with former pupils were sustained through the Old Students' Association of the Grammar School. They attended every meeting of the association and loved to hear about the members' lives, families and achievements.

Some three years ago, when it became too difficult for them to continue in their own house, they moved to St Mary's Nursing Home at Ednaston. Sadly, Grace died a year later. The last two years have been comfortable for Kathleen, cared for by the staff at Ednaston and visited regularly by friends.

The lives of many Derbeians have been enriched by Kathleen and Grace. We shall always remember them with admiration and affection.

Cynthia Marks (former colleague), Allestree.

Derby Evening Telegraph – Tuesday 19th March 2002 by Cynthia Marks

HOMELANDS OLD GIRLS' ASSOCIATION

HOMELANDS SCHOOL PLAYS

Spring 1947 – Le Cid

Kathleen Garner Dora Bexson Sheila Richards

Spring 1948 – Le Malade Imaginaire

Hazel Aitchison Yvonne Maurer Olive Hames Diana Earp Betty Hill Mayze Melville Rhona Wilson
Sheila Stowe Jean Turner Sheila Richards

Dora Bexson Joan Lawrence Jean Turner

Dora Bexon Unknown Kathleen Garner Jean Turner Unknown

Kate Goodchild Kathleen Garner Olive Hames Joan Lawrence Dora Bexon Betty Wallace Jean Turner

Photographs courtesy of Marjorie Calow

SPEECH DAY

Thursday, January 20th, 1949
at 2.30 p.m.

Distribution of Prizes and Certificates

by

B. L. HALLWARD, ESQ., M.A.
Vice-Chancellor of The University of Nottingham

Chairman :

COUNCILLOR MRS. E. E. ARMSTRONG
Chairman of the School Governors

PROGRAMME

Song. ... ... "Torrents in Summer"—*Elgar* ... ... The School

---

CHAIRMAN'S OPENING REMARKS.
REPORT BY THE HEAD MISTRESS.

Song. ... "A Lake and a Fairy Boat"—*Dunhill* ... Senior Choir

---

DISTRIBUTION OF PRIZES AND CERTIFICATES BY
B. L. HALLWARD, ESQ., M.A.

School Orchestra—

Three Songs by Brahms (arr. C. Woodhouse)—

"The Little Sandman"

"Lullaby"

"The Blacksmith"

ADDRESS.

Songs. ... ... "Trees in England"—*Charles Wood* ... Junior Choir

"A Carrion Crow"—*Paul Edmonds*

VOTE OF THANKS.

School Song. "Non Nobis Domine"—*Roger Quilter* ... ... The School

---

NATIONAL ANTHEM.

PRIZE LIST - 1947-48

Form Prizes. (For effort and achievement in all subjects throughout the year).

I.	Jacqueline Brindley.	Betty Old.	Patricia Townley.
	Denise Goddard.	Anne Shirley.	Audrey Watson.
	Valerie Holmes.		
II.	Pamela Cheney.	Gwendoline Fawkes.	Pamela Ludlow.
	Margaret Cocker.	Eva Lee.	Theresa Timperley.
	Jean Dallison.		
III.	Celia Brookes.	Margaret Hodson.	Patricia Ottewell.
	Shirley Greenwood.	Sheila Mosses.	Sheila States.
	Christine Hird.	Barbara Newns.	
IV.	Brenda Atkinson.	June Handley.	Margaret Wallace.
	Jean Castledine.	Sonia Holland.	Valerie Wallwin.
	Joyce Fenton.	Olive Morley.	Patricia Whyte.
	Pamela Gibson.	Margaret Tong.	

L. V. Barbara Dyche. Rosalie Hare. Patricia Slater. Frances Stringer
V. Prizes for gaining good School Certificates.
L. VI. Advanced Work Prizes :

Patricia L'Estrange ... Latin and French.
Kate Goodchild ... French.
Olive Hames ... French.
Joan Lawrence ... Geography.
Vera Seago ... Science.
Sheila Bell ... Matriculation.
Yvonne Maurer ... Matriculation.
Mollie Lewis ... Preliminary State Nursing Examination, Part I.

VI. Mary McLean ... Oxford Entrance in English.
Prizes for gaining a full Higher School Certificate.

EXAMINATION SUCCESSES - 1947-48

London University Higher School Examination.

Arts :

Dora Bexson ... Special Credit in Oral French, English, French, Modern History.
Kathleen Garner ... Special Credit in Oral French, English, French, Modern History.
Patricia Hawkes ... English, French, Modern History.
Barbara Hull ... English, Modern History, Geography, Art.
Jean Lilley ... English, French, Modern History.
Sheila Richards ... English with Distinction, French with Distinction and Special Credit in Oral, Modern History. Subsidiary—Latin. Exemption from London Intermediate Arts.
Stella Southam ... English, French, Music.
Sheila Stowe ... English, Geography. Subsidiary—Art, Music.
Joyce Swain ... Modern History with Distinction, English, Art. Subsidiary—Religious Knowledge.
Barbara Toone ... English, French, Modern History.
Jean Turner ... Special Credit in Oral French, Latin, French, Modern History.
Elizabeth Wallace... French with Distinction and Special Credit in Oral, English, Modern History. Subsidiary—Latin. Exemption from London Intermediate Arts.

Science :

Celia Hullah ... Physics, Pure Mathematics, Zoology. Exemption from London Intermediate Science.
Anne Webster ... Physics, Pure Mathematics, Applied Mathematics. Exemption from London Intermediate Science.

Not entered for Full Examination :

Jean Davison ... Art. Mary Knights ... Art. Doreen Lindon ... Art.

London University General School Examination.

(A "Very Good" mark was gained in the subjects in brackets).

December, 1947.

General School Certificate with Matriculation Exemption :
Yvonne Maurer (History).

General School Certificate :
Ruth Dyson. Marion Lee. Jean Murfin.
Margaret Jones. Mollie Lewis.

Additional Subjects :
Sheila Bell. Eve Pendrill (Chemistry).
Mayze Melville, giving Matriculation exemption. Muriel Wright.

July, 1948.

General School Certificate with Matriculation Exemption :

Joan Barker.	Dorothy Perkins (French).
Sheila Bell.	Margaret Stanley (French).
Shirley Briggs (History, French).	Olive Tate.
Patricia Broadbent (History).	Joan Watkinson.
Joan Brown (French).	June Allen (Art).
Marjorie Calow (English, English Literature, History, French, General Science).	Agnes Brown (History).
	Thelma Cook.
	Sheila Gallimore (French).
Marian Hall.	Margaret Holmes.
Jean Hardy (History, French, Elementary Mathematics).	Barbara Hale (Geography, Art).
	Myra Thompson (French, Art).
Audrey Menzies.	Jean Willatt.

General School Certificate :

Valerie Buxton.	Mary Blower.	Margaret Smith.
Stella Clarricoats.	(History).	Barbara Stevens (French).
Brenda Crofts (History).	Sheila Castledine.	Anne Tennett.
Margaret Flatt.	Sally Cooper (History).	Marjorie Willows.
Audrey Hine (English).	Sheila Corner.	Sheila Wright.
	June Coxon (Art).	Thelma Bartley.
Elizabeth Maddocks.	Irene Hallsworth.	Eileen Blackshields.
Joyce Mercer (History, Geography, French).	Sylvia Haslam (French).	Marjorie Bown.
	Audrey Haveron.	Sylvia Churchman.
	Margaret Jarman.	Lilian Cope.
Jean Shardlow.	Grace McLean (French).	Betty Cullen.
Jean Steeples.	Margaret Osborne (History).	Rita Payne.
June Bembridge.		Shirley Piggs.
Joan Bircher.	Ivy Shaw.	Margaret Sinclair (History).
		Pamela Walton.
		Ruth Wells.

Successes in Additional Subjects :

Gwendolene Allen.	Margaret Jones.	Mary Lowe.
Jean Davison.	Audrey Kemp.	Jean Murfin.
Moyra Harrison.	Patricia L'Estrange (Latin).	Vera Seago (Chemistry).
Betty Hill, giving Matriculation exemption.	Mollie Lewis.	Brenda Shreeve.
	Doreen Lindon.	Joan White.

SCHOLARSHIPS.

State Scholarship ... ... Sheila Richards.
Reserve List ... ... Elizabeth Wallace.
Borough Major Scholarship ... ... Sheila Richards.
Drapers' Scholarship ... ... Jean Turner.

UNIVERSITY ENTRANCE.

Oxford ... Somerville College ... ... Mary McLean.
St. Anne's Society ... ... Jean Turner.
... ... Elizabeth Wallace.

London ... King's College of Household and
Social Science ... ... Eve Pendrill.

Royal College of Music ... ... Stella Southam.
Trinity College of Music ... ... Sheila Stowe.

Preliminary State Nursing Examination (Part I).
Mollie Lewis.

London City & Guilds—Needlework (Class II). Barbara Hull.

Quiet schoolmistress shapes the future for 600 girls

At 7 her aim in life was clear...

Victor Head interviews....

Miss M.P. Helmore

Erect as a pillar in her well-cut tweeds, and viewing the Universe with a faintly disapproving air from under her sensible, multi-season hat, the traditional English schoolmarm has marched all over modern literature and established herself in a permanent supporting role on the world's stage.

Miss Margery Phyllis Helmore, as sketched by the Alvaston artist, A. Morton.

In real life, of course, such archetypes are hard to discover. Instead, you will find an astonishing variety of gifted persons who have dedicated themselves to teaching. Meet, for example, Miss Margery Phyllis Helmore, who has been Headmistress of Homelands Grammar School for Girls, Derby, since 1947.

Whether she is walking up moderate-sized mountains while on holiday in the Pyrenees; occupying an idle moment learning a new language; or directing a full-scale costume production at the school of Barrie's 'Quality Street,' Miss Helmore's energy and enthusiasm are boundless.

All this drive is concealed behind a quiet, almost placid personality, that inspires confidence in parents and affection in pupils.

Under her care are 600 prospective nurses, teachers, scientists, engineers, artists, secretaries, housewives – the list is as long as you care to make it, so wide is the choice open to the girls with a Homelands School training behind them.

To lead them along the thorny paths of learning, direct them towards the careers for which they seem best fitted, and at the same time harmonise relations between staff and parents, explain objectives and share in settling day-to-day administrative problems between staff and education authority, is a task that calls for the patience of Job and his wisdom of Solomon.

Early decision

Fortunately Miss Helmore is one of those selfless, devoted souls who form the backbone of the English teaching profession. At the age of seven she announced to the family circle that she was going to be a schoolteacher. She probably decided privately that nothing short of a headmistress's post would suffice, but she kept that information to herself.

Such single-mindedness of purpose brought its own reward with her appointment at Homelands in 1947, but the road to this pinnacle was a long one, full of hard work and the necessary acquisition of experience.

Born in Devon 53 years ago Miss Helmore clear-eyed candour one associates with West Country folk. She was educated at Bishop Blackall School for Girls, then at her own Exeter University, where she was a scholar and won the coveted Franklin prize. Later at London University she obtained her M.A. in English with distinction.

Twice her career brought her into this district before she came to Homelands. Her job was at Sutton-in-Ashfield Secondary School. Where, incidentally, her love of amateur theatricals led her to form the local amateur dramatics society and become its first organising secretary.

We next see her in Derbyshire at the beginning of the war, when she came to Chapel-en-le-Frith with the evacuated Westcliff High School, as head of its English Department. With 650 students this was at that time one of the largest girl's schools in the country, and her experience at Westcliff proved invaluable training for the task and responsibilities that lay ahead.

Miss Helmore's interest in the theatre has never flagged and when she came to Derby she herself produced many of the school plays.

She leaves this task to her staff now, without ever quite resisting the temptation to look in at rehearsals and offer advice.

School aims

Miss Helmore's attitude to her job is, perhaps, best revealed in one at her own annual reports. In it she describes her aims for her girls as 'sound learning, thoroughness and exactness, delight in work for work's sake, and the pursuit of truth and knowledge.'

All these, she says, are possible without examinations, particularly in a society impressed with the value of education.

'But in a society where monetary and material values rank high,' she continues, 'the award of a certificate is a most useful incentive'.

'Education with the wrong motive is better than no education at all.'

Derby Evening Telegraph – Friday 22nd May 1959

It's goodbye to 'Miss Homelands'
Last of the original staff to retire

MISS LOYDALL – she came to Homelands when the school opened

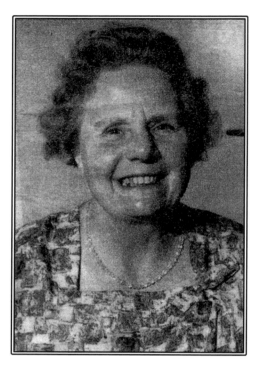

TWO factors have influenced the life of Miss F. Evelyn Loydall, Deputy Headmistress of Homelands School, Derby – her devotion and loyalty to the school, and Spain's fascination for her.

Her loyalty to Homelands has kept her there since the school opened in 1938, moving from the former Central School for Girls, which formed the nucleus of Homelands. Before that she taught in junior schools in the town for two years after gaining a degree in French at Nottingham University College, now Nottingham University.

The last one

And when she retires as Deputy Head at the end of term, she will not sever her connections with Homelands.

Miss Loydall's interest in the theatre and amateur dramatics will take her back for the school's dramatic society productions, with which she has been connected for many years.

Miss Loydall of 107 Elms Avenue, Littleover, has been Deputy Headmistress for seven years, and has served under all four headmistresses. She will be the last original member of the staff to retire.

To Madrid

For many years she taught French, but as her interest in Spain grew, so did her interest in the language, and after completing a course in Spanish, she decided to teach the language. She attended courses all over the country, and in Madrid, and gained a London degree.

Miss Loydall began teaching the language at Homelands five years ago and is extremely pleased by the results gained by pupils. 'I have found that girls who take Spanish did better than they would have done in French,' she says.

124

Her love for Spain began in 1947 when the frontier between France and Spain was opened for the first time in ten years. 'It was like stepping back into another world, and I was very impressed by the Moorish influence.'

Since 1951 Miss Loydall has taken parties of girls for a holiday in San Sebastian, on several occasions.

Spanish people, she finds are most friendly towards the British. And bull-fighting, the national sport of the Spaniards, has as much an emotional and exciting effect on her as it does on them.

'To see a man so close to death is what makes it so attractive to the Spaniards. But the sport is being kept alive by the tourists,' she said.

Miss Loydall has a collection of 100 Spanish dolls, and buys one in every town she visits. She also has a vast collection of items of Spanish crafts, and, with the dolls, illustrates the talks on Spain she gives to local organisations.

Holiday first

Miss Loydall is looking forward to a full and happy retirement. 'I intend to rest, and to enjoy myself, beginning with a holiday in Ibiza in September when most of the tourists have gone home,' she laughed.

'I am going to read the books I want to read, and if I get bored, which is doubtful, I will learn German.'

She also intends to carry on telling the people of Derby all about Spain.

Miss Loydall's class at Homelands Grammar School, Derby, in the 1950s.

Photograph courtesy of Derby Evening Telegraph

Derby Evening Telegraph

Former grammar school head dies

Mrs Joyce Allman who served as a teacher under Miss Helmore said: 'Her whole life was the school, she was interested in all her pupils and the teachers. She knew everybody by name, and followed the careers of her pupils after they left.'

In loving memory of Margery Phyllis Helmore

Born in Exeter 19 May 1905 – Died in Bealey 8 December 1981

THE news of the death of Miss Margery Helmore, former headteacher of Homelands School, Derby, marks the passing of an era

She was in charge of the all-girls grammar school in the days when to the pupils came headmistress was 'God' and her word law.

I was never clever, so I always felt Miss Helmore regarded me as one of her failures. She often had to chide me about not wearing my school hat, not working as hard as she felt I could and inevitably talking too much.

Yet later when I had begun a career in journalism I met her again when I returned to the old school to cover speech day for the local newspaper.

Then I discovered that far from being the nonentity I was sure she must have thought me, she had followed my career with great interest and even mentioned articles I had written and almost forgotten myself.

Since she retired to live in north Derbyshire, of course the whole face of education has altered.

I doubt that she would have liked the changes – a mixed comprehensive as Homelands now is, somehow just wouldn't seem the right place for her.

She wasn't one of those headteachers girls idolise, but in a quiet way she contributed a great deal to the lives of many women in Derby, though it wasn't until much later in life that some of us realised the debt we owed her and her staff.

Derby Trader – Wednesday 16th December 1981

Grammar school girls take trip back in time

Former pupils publish a booklet of memories

Margaret Baxter, Marjorie Calow, Stella Allen and Joyce Varty

Photograph courtesy of Derby Evening Telegraph

COMMUNAL showers, the smell of chemistry rooms and French grammar are all part of the collective memories of a group of ex pupils of a former Derby school.

Their recollections of schooldays in the 1940s were stirred with the closure of Village Community School, Normanton, two years ago.

Now they have decided to put their memories into written form and have produced a 64-page booklet about their schooldays.

They remember the school as Homelands Grammar School for Girls, in Village Street, and they were among the first pupils to be educated there after it opened in the late 1930s.

The school was closed by the city council after pupil numbers fell over the last few years.

Although the former pupils have kept in touch over the years since they left the school, it was after they met at the final open day before it closed that the idea for the booklet was conceived.

The women – Marjorie Calow, Stella Allen (nee Clarricoats), Margaret Baxter (nee Flatt), June Allen and Joyce Varty (nee Mercer) – have written their own individual recollections of their school lives.

These have been put together, with photographs of the school and themselves as pupils, along with copies of speech day programmes.

Mrs Calow, of Melbourne said: 'We were saddened by the closure of the school. We enjoyed producing the booklet, and we hope that it means that our wonderful school will not be forgotten.'

Almost all of the women recall their horror of having to take showers after PE, but they all thoroughly enjoyed their school days despite some fearsome teachers.

Mrs Calow recalled: 'A good gymnast always sits up straight!' These words put the fear of God into me! The speaker was Miss Hilda Land and it was my first day at the school in 1942.

'I was sitting in the dinning room and I must have been picked on because I was slouching. Gym and games lessons were torture.'

But her experiences did not put her off, for as Mrs Calow reveals in the booklet, she later returned to the school as chemistry mistress.

She said: 'It was strange to be on the staff with people who had taught me, but they were wonderful, dedicated women.'

Stella Allen was also impressed with the school and recalls her first days of being surrounded by polish, new furniture and books.

She said: 'My needlework took me ages to complete and always ended up grubby with too tight stitching!'

Derby Evening Telegraph – Monday 3rd March 2003 by Zena Hawley

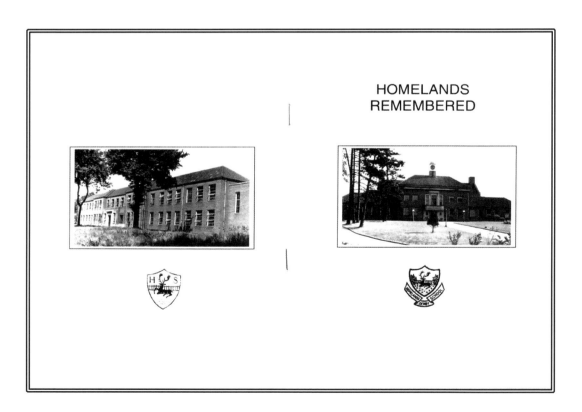

Back Cover – Rear of Homeland School   Front Cover – Front of Homelands School

From school mistress to union militant

BORN in Melbourne, Marjorie Calow was the daughter of George Calow, a skilled craftsman, a funeral director, and evidently a man of many parts. Marjorie speaks of him as being 'an archetypal liberal non-conformist, self educated skilled craftsman', a man who was determined that his daughter should have a good education.

As Marjorie comments 'There were many families who could not afford for their children to have a good education, as they were required to work, as soon as the school leaving age was reached.'

She went to Homelands, a Grammar School, and eventually to London to study Chemistry, which in those days, in 1950, for a young woman of her background was unusual. She got her degree, and was immediately asked to go back to Homelands, to teach Chemistry.

In a booklet 'Homelands Remembered', which Marjorie edited in 2002, she speaks of very happy schooldays, except for the hatred of gym and sports. Marjorie now exercises most assiduously by walking at least 90 minutes each day, and many will have seen her walking in and around Melbourne.

Her home in Melbourne now is the home of an academic, books lining every space on every wall, CDs in profusion, and she is plainly a woman of many interests, in literature, in politics, in history, and in feminism. She had a scientific education but speaks ruefully of C.P. Snow's Two Cultures, and the fact that she had a lot of catching up to do to introduce herself to the world outside science.

Married after graduation, Marjorie taught for less than three years at Homelands, and then joined the company where her husband then worked. Boots the Chemist, in Beeston. Her account of her 22 years at Boots is a saga of her awaking to the injustices that were then the norm for women at work.

She was employed as an analytical chemist. 'It was the unfairness and the injustice that I suggested at work that made me politicised and unionised,' said Marjorie.

'I was a square peg in a round hole at Boots,' but she kept sane in those early days at Boots, as she continued to educate herself at the Adult Education Centre in Nottingham. Increasingly however the sense of injustice at the unequal way women were treated at work incensed her.

She was barred from entry to the Pension Fund, because she was married, and then she began to ask more questions. Of the 22 years she worked at Boots, only seven were pensionable, which has resulted in her having a retirement 'in relative penury'. It is difficult for men today to realise that women were so seriously discriminated against.

At Boots in the 1950s and 1960s, women got paid less than men, for the same work, men got more holidays, because holiday entitlement was based on salary.

Women were never promoted, and their Unions 'did not want to know about the discrimination.'

So Marjorie became unionised herself, eventually became branch secretary of the union, ASTMS, and her beliefs were hardened by reading *The Female Eunach*, and *The Feminine Mystique*. She quickly became involved at both Divisional and National level.

Marjorie took a decisive step in 1978, when she left Boots, to read for a Master's degree in Industrial relations at Warwick University. From there she became an employee of the WEA (Workers' Educational Association), specialising in women's studies, teaching and organising, and ending up responsible for Women's studies throughout the East Midlands, as well as teaching courses for the TUC.

Marjorie completed a third degree in English Literature, at the Open University. She was a lady member of Industrial Tribunals, and finally retired from the WEA in 1991. Marjorie's marriage ended in a civilised manner. 'We are still very good friends,' and she lives in retirement in her father's house.

Her work with the WEA have a great deal of satisfaction, particularly as her father had been all his life an ardent supporter of the movement. Apart from her walking, she has interests and many friends. She's certainly is a most interesting person to talk to, with a wide range of interests, presumably, because with a science training, and subsequent broad education, she had successfully crossed over the great Two Culture divide.

She holds strong political views – not any longer a Labour supporter, after the Iraq invasion. But she had lost none of her faith that women must be developed to their full potential, and that 'I believe very strongly in the desirability of financial independence for women.'

Village Voice – December 2003

Homelands Remembered

'One of my more pleasant duties during the last year of Village, formerly Homelands, School, was to take several groups of "old girls" on a tour of the school and to organise an evening when such archives as we had found were put on display for past pupils before being either sent to the Matlock Archives or "skipped".

I felt some nervousness before the first of those tours, one of which included Marjorie Calow and her friends, because of the painful discrepancy between the school's character and aspirations when it was founded in the 30s and its very different character and impending demise in 2001. Having taken up the post of Head teacher there in 1998, determined to prove what an inner city school could achieve even in the most challenging circumstances, I soon discovered that discussions about its closure were far advanced and my job became largely that of sustaining the education of the pupils there during the two years' consultation and closure process.

The visits of former pupils were great fun, though. The corridors and classrooms stimulated instant recall: who sat where and next to whom; what happened when; which teacher taught there ... the intervening decades visibly slipped away! I particularly remember one visitor's story of life in the air raid shelters during the war, where a bucket was kept behind a curtain at one end of the shelter for use as a toilet, and how the teachers would lead the girls in singing songs to cover any embarrassing noises whenever a girl needed to make use of it. We all wondered whether today's children would be so considerate, or whether similar nudges and comments would have been made even then, despite the singing.

There is a sadness when your old school closes. It must be rather like seeing the home you grew up in being bulldozed. We like these linchpins of our childhood to remain constant years after we have left them, as if we don't want our own youth to leave us. Well, memories of childhood and school days certainly haven't left the seven contributors to "Homelands Remembered". The recollections are fresh and vivid, spiced with humorous anecdotes and some frank admissions. For anyone who was at the school and remembers the teachers, buildings, speech days and showers with affection or horror, it is not to be missed. For others, it is an entertaining read, which will rekindle universal memories of childhood and school days.

As to whether education has changed for better or worse since then, that's quite a separate issue!'

Edward Gildea

Melbourne Civic Society

Protecting and improving the environment of Melbourne Derbyshire since 1974

Melbourne Civic Society Newsletter – No 117 – October 2002

Honours Boards

Photograph courtesy of K. S. Dhindsa © 2017

It is my hope that any profit generated from the sales of this book will be used to:

• Restore the Homelands Grammar School for Girls Honours Boards and find them a permanent home

• Erect a Homelands plaque at the old school's site on Village Street, Derby.

Homelands Plaque

Designer

Tamás Miklós Fülep

Sculptor

Andrew Edwards

Introduction

'Homelands From The Beginning'

1938–43

I was pleased to read the excellent booklet, *Homelands Remembered* compiled by seven Old Girls who began their secondary school life in 1943. However, I felt that there were some earlier anecdotes, which should be reordered. In Homelands Remembered I was pleased to see on the middle pages the ground and first floor plans of Homelands School. Also, I am grateful to Dorothy Padmore née Perkins for the history of Homelands House.

Regarding the Guest Speaker at Speech Days – once we were addressed by a lady called Dr Consett. She spoke for a long time so we nicknamed her Dr Can't Sit!

Thank you to twelve of my contemporaries who began at Homelands in 1938 and who sent their reminiscences to me. There were some events that were recalled by several contributors. In the interests of variety I have rarely repeated such topics.

Winifred (née Eales) Curzon

September 2004

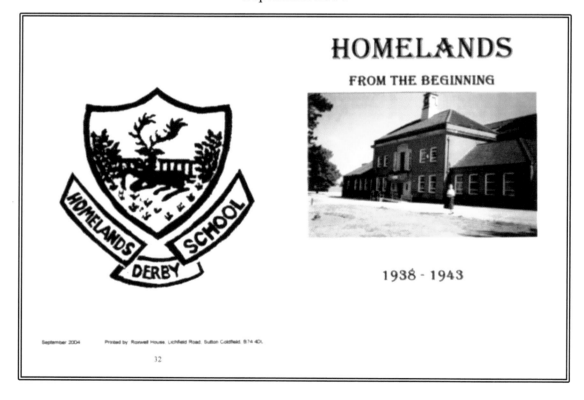

HOMELANDS

FROM THE BEGINNING

1938 - 1943

September 2004   Printed by Ronwell House, Lichfield Road, Sutton Coldfield, B74 4DL.

32

Editorial Team

Winifred Curzon   Ray and Sybil Brant

I thank Winifred for putting our story together, also to her daughter Jane for doing the printing.

However we have since had more contributions, and now it is my husband Ray and myself to put it together. He with the computer and me with the sorting out.

The colour photograph below of the 1993 reunion shows Miss Loydall (wearing a blue and white dress) in the centre of the front row.

ALLSOP Joan   COMPTON Marion   FOXON Margaret   HOLLAND Norma
ASHTON June   CUTTS Jean   GAWTHROP Audrey   HOLMES Muriel
BALDWIN Beryl   DOLMAN Iris   HALL Margaret   JAMES Betty
BEARDMORE Noreen EALES Winifred   HARLOW Florence   LOWE Irene
BEZANT Joy   FAZEY Alma   HARRISON Rosemary OTTEWELL Sybil
BRAY Sheila   FENTON Audrey   HARTROFF Kathleen RAWLINGS Marian
BROMLEY Audrey   FOX Betty   HIND Kathleen   RECORD Doris

Friday, June 11th 1993

RISBY Pat   SMITH Gina   TIBBERT Veronica WIBBERLEY Mavis
SHEPARD Patricia STONE Connie   TINKLER Beryl   WIBBERLEY Pat
SMEDLEY Kathleen THOMPSON Sheila TOON Lydia   WALL Janet

Introduction

'Homelands Remembered'

Last night I dreamt of Homelands … Some of us occasionally dream about Homelands and some of us have sharp memories of our schooldays – or think we do. When seven 'old girls', saddened by the closure of the school, took the decision to commit our memories to paper, independently and without collaboration, several of us remembered the same incidents, but from rather different perspectives. We have enjoyed producing this booklet and hope, at the very least, it will ensure our wonderful school is not totally forgotten.

Marjorie Calow

Summer 2002

Dorothy (left) and Marjorie working on Homelands Remembered, March 2002

Photograph courtesy of Margaret Baxter

We acknowledge, with gratitude, the help we have received from Robin Lewis (Solicitor), Michael Moore (Education Service, Derby City Council), Philip Heath (Heritage Officer, South Derbyshire District Council), Edward Gildea (Head Teacher of the School in its last days before closure) and Wendy Nuttall (Marco Business Centre).

Kalwinder Singh Dhindsa

Attended 'The Village Community School' from September 1991 to July 1996.

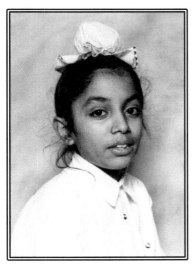

'I loved Village Community School. What more can I say? Yes, I knew it had a bad reputation for achievement and discipline before, during and after my time there. However, the people I associated myself with at school all just wanted to do well. My own little group of friends would compete against each other on friendly terms to outdo each other and that's what carried us all through. I didn't see it as a bad school. We just made the best of what we had there and I would like to think that those of us who really cared about our education gave it our all and always gave it our best. I definitely left the school feeling indebted to it and all the great teachers who had done so much for us all over the years. It was a great shame when it closed its doors forever.'

From 'My Father & The Lost Legend of Pear Tree – Part One' by Kalwinder Singh Dhindsa

Tamás Miklós Fülep

Attended 'Normanton Secondary School / Homelands Comprehensive School' from September 1971 to July 1976.

'I didn't take my drawing or education seriously through my youth. My artwork at school definitely caught the attention of teachers, but only because they were often the subjects. I made my classmates laugh though. Having a laugh was my general attitude towards school and I left in 1976 with a CSE in art as my main qualification. My art teacher forcefully encouraged me to go onto art college, but I just didn't want to spend any more years in a classroom. I still continue freelancing to this day, but the more I use traditional tools, pencils and brushes, the more I enjoy my work. As I approach my sixties I have just one more objective in my working life, to try and establish myself as just an "artist".'

KALEIDOSCOPE HOUSE

Neighbours fume over mural mix

by Paul Trueman

● TOM FULEP, poised with brush and paint set, beside the giant mural at his Sinfin home.

VAN driver Tom Fulep's attempts to brighten up his Derby home with a work of art have been given the brush-off by neighbours who are seeing red over the rainbow-coloured house.

The front wall is painted in bands of blue, green, yellow, orange, red and purple. Over the front door is a collection of large models, such as a Coca Cola tin and a container from which have a leg with a fishnet stocking and high heel shoe sticks out.

There is even a lavatory seat with a message inside it which says "Why Not?"

Job hope

On the large gable end wall Tom (26), of 127 Shakespeare Street, Sinfin, has painted a huge mural in bright colours depicting among other things, a liner, the statue of Liberty, the Sphinx and Big Ben.

Mr. Fulep said: "I just like to be different. I have always wanted to be different.

"I have always been interested in art, particularly graphic art.

"I thought it would brighten the place up."

There is also a serious side to the display . . . he is hoping it will land him a job as an artist.

"I've been approached by the local parish council to do some murals for them and by somebody else to decorate a float for Derby carnival," he said.

There has been a mixed reaction from Tom's neighbours.

Mr. Steve Winter, of 24 Cowper Street, says: "This art has been inflicted and forced upon us. To me it is just graffiti and it stands out, like a sore thumb."

Mr. Winter, like his artistic neighbour, is buying his council home.

"What annoys me is that the ordinary member of the public can't do anything about it."

His wife, Fay, commented: "We have complained to Derby City Council and I'm thoroughly disgusted that the council has done nothing about it."

Across the road Mr. Ken Johnson, of 15 Cowper Street, who faces the giant mural every time he looks out of his front window, commented: "It's good but I don't think it is the right place for it."

Mrs. Denise Simpson (34), of 124 Shakespeare Street, said: "I have no objection. It's better than looking at bare walls.

"I think he's got guts to do it."

Replying to the critics, Mr. Fulep said: "It's everbody to their own taste and this is my taste."

His wife, Deborah (23), said: "I think it is good and it helps to brighten up the place."

Mr. Steve Barry, Sinfin area housing manager for Derby City Council, said today: "The housing department has only limited powers because the chap is an owner-occupier. We are looking into the matter, from the planning aspect to see whether planning permission was needed.

"As yet we have received no formal complaints but as soon as we do we will take them very seriously."

Council set to resolve house mural dispute

by John Wilson

CITY council officials are to confront Derby mural man Mr Tom Fulep over his multi-coloured home.

The artistic van driver's ecentric attempts to brighten up his home have turned the air blue in Sinfin's Shakespeare Street.

Some of his furious neighbours have written protest letters to the city council about Mr Fulep's extrovert artwork.

No breach

Now council chiefs are set to meet him to thrash out a solution to the problem.

Mr Steve Barry, Sinfin area housing manager for Derby City Council, said Mr Fulep's multi-coloured murals did not breach local planning regulations.

"Although Mr Fulep has not broken any regulations we have had some complaints about his house so council staff will be visiting him to try to sort something out," he explained.

Mr Fulep's wife Deborah (23) said the couple would be willing to listen to what the council officials had to say.

But she added: "We're not too worried about what's happening because all the publicity has done a world of good. He's already had offers of painting jobs and an art magazine has been taking an interest in what he has done."

Mr Fulep (26) will begin painting a mural for the City's Cock and Bull pub in the next couple of weeks.

Mr Fulep's former council house at 127 Shakespeare Street has been painted from top to bottom in the colours of the rainbow.

Large murals adorn the gable end, a rainbow stretches across the front wall and a giant Cocoa Cola tin nestles over the front door.

Articles courtesy of Derby Evening Telegraph

New career for Tom the mural man

ARTISTIC van driver, Tom Fulep, has drawn up plans to launch his own colourful business enterprise.

The eccentric mural man's attempts to brighten up his home in Derby's Shakespeare Street hit the headlines when neighbours protested.

But despite their complaints Tom (26) is on cloud nine.

All the publicity about his extrovert artwork has brought him a flood of offers to put his talents to work elsewhere in the city.

Now Tom is all set to give up his job and strike out on his own as a freelance artist.

"All the publicity has done me a world of good. The work keeps rolling in," he said.

Tom's former council house at 127 Shakespeare Street, Sinfin, has been painted from top to bottom in the colours of the rainbow.

by Telegraph Reporters

Large murals adorn the gable end, a rainbow stretches across the front wall and a giant Coca Cola tin nestles over the front door.

Said Tom: "I've got plenty of work in the pipeline and I could get more, but with a full-time job I just haven't got time.

"I've always wanted to set up on my own and all the publicity surrounding the house has given me the incentive to do it."

Tom has already completed four orders for murals, which will be his speciality when he launches his business.

He has already got his scheme moving by painting "Tom the Mural Man" and his telephone number on his car.

'Nixon Jeans'
Abbey Street, Derby

Photograph courtesy of Derby Evening Telegraph

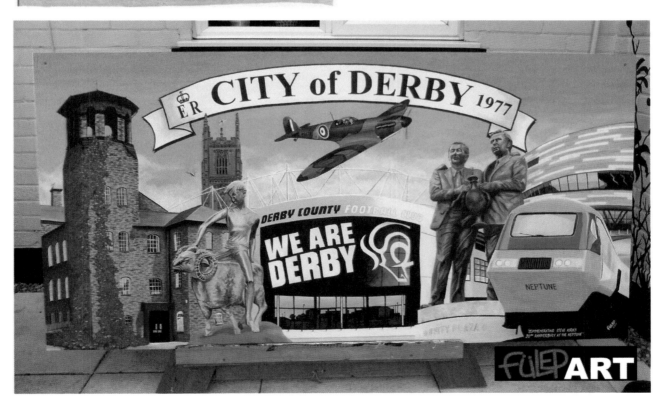

'City of Derby'
Neptune Pub, Osmaston Road, Derby

www.fulep.com

Special Thanks

Derby 🐏 Telegraph

Normanton-by-Derby: The Story of a Village

Compiled by Members of the Normanton-by-Derby Local History Group and Friends

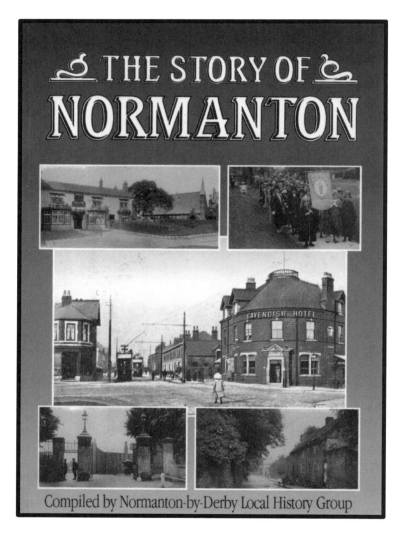

Contributors

Ron Adamson Audrey Bate Norma Consterdine Leslie Cox
Phyllis Oldknow Joyce Poynton Judith Raven Michael Shaw
Peter & Eileen Thompson

Coming Soon

'Homelands Reclaimed'

'Homelands Reclaimed' will be a collection of memories from ex-students, teachers, support staff and anyone else associated with 'Homelands'

Homelands Grammar School for Girls

Homelands Comprehensive School

Normanton Secondary School

Village Community School

Village High School

1938 – 2002

Printed in Great Britain
by Amazon